TOGETHER for CHRISTMAS

A resource anthology

CHURCH INFORMATION OFFICE
Church House, Dean's Yard, Westminster, SW1P 3NZ

A

ISBN 0 7151 0366 0

Published for the General Synod Board of Education 1975
Third reprint 1981

Printed in England by Loxley Brothers Limited, Sheffield

CONTENTS

	page
Foreword	5
Pageants, Plays and Services	
A Festival of Christmas Customs	7
A Play for All Seasons	15
The Little White Inn	20
Down to Earth	24
What on Earth . . . ?	28
If Christ were born on Tees-side	34
The 'Zither Carol' Mime	38
How Far is it to Bethlehem?	40
Rest on the Flight	48
The Twelve Reporters	53
The Christmas Bellman	55
A Cause for Carols	60
The First Christmas Tree	63
Jesus is King	66
'No Room . . .'	69
Christmas Eve, 1818	79
The Wood Speaks	81
'Jesus is Alive!'	89
'Standing in the Rain . . .'	96
Prayers and Poems	
Three Prayers for Christmas	98
Seasonal Prayers	100
So Green the Ash	102
A Carol of his Coming	103
Advent in a Stable	104
The Witnesses	105
Jesus Today	106
The Heart of the Apple	107
To Bethlehem with Love	108
Point of no Returning	109
Three Christmas Songs	110
Things to do and make	
A Simple Crib	112
Crafts for Christmas	115

FOREWORD

Round about early October there gathers on the teacher's horizon—whether that teacher works in day or Sunday school, with tots of five or ambitious 13-year olds—a cloud no bigger than a man's hand. It is the need to 'find something new for Christmas', to interpret afresh so well-known a story in terms that make sense to today's children.

For the past few years this cloud has been slightly lifted for those teachers who subscribe to *Together*, the magazine of the General Synod Board of Education, published for all who are concerned in religious education. Other teachers, group leaders and clergy send to *Together* those ideas which they have put into practice with children and found to work. Now we have decided that instead of sending out back numbers of our magazine every autumn to the many enquirers who write in looking for Christmas material, we will collect into book form some of the best-liked plays, services, poems, carols and craftwork that have appeared in its pages.

We would stress that these are only ideas—suggestions upon which to build. Please don't feel that they must be copied word for word; we simply offer them as models. If you feel, 'We could do something much better with that idea', then take the plunge, go ahead and do it. It will be better, because it will be yours and your children's. Similarly if you are not happy about the particular carols recommended substitute those of your own choice.

If we can help with our suggestions, we are happy. If you are left still searching, don't despair. Beyond the cloud is a star. Beyond all the fuss and rehearsals and let-downs and crises, beyond the old ladies who like it traditional, the parents who yearn for angels in white nighties and the colleagues who want only a secular celebration, there is the good moment—the moment when we realise afresh, every Christmas, that 'the light shines on in the darkness and the darkness has not overcome it'.

Happy Christmas!

Pamela Egan
Editor, *Together*

A FESTIVAL OF CHRISTMAS CUSTOMS

Tydfil Roberts wrote for an infant school this pageant in which every child can take part

'*Not* another carol service on the same pattern as hundreds of others. *Not* another nativity play with a selected few lisping their way artificially through rehearsed speeches which have grown stale by the day of the performance.'

Such were the two main thoughts going through my mind as Christmas gradually neared. But yet I wanted something within which the children could enjoy themselves and yet identify themselves with the Nativity of our Lord through their singing, their dancing, their acting, their ears and their eyes.

One little girl showed me a Christmas recipe book. That, of all things, was my starting point. This little offering evolved from something as simple as that. (Evolved is the right word, for suggestions for many parts came from the children themselves.) Of one thing I was certain: every child had to be involved. No one was too big or too small, too tone deaf or too clumsy to be involved in some way. This is the reason why there is no definite number of characters in the play.

To all who play this piece, I wish the same delight and joy that we had.

Characters

1 Narrator throughout, or 16 narrators taken in turn from the choir.

Nativity tableau:

Joseph
Mary (with doll)
3 shepherds
3 wise men
1 or more angels

Choir: all the rest of the children. At various stages in the play certain members of the choir will also be:

- 2 boys with sledge of holly
- 1 boy with lighted taper
- 6 carol singers
- 1 decoration box holder
- 1 postman
- 12 poster bearers (or 2 frieze-holders, if there is a shortage of children)
- 5 cooks
- 1 Father Christmas.

The stage

An extremely simple set is required, merely a series of steps to the right of the stage for the nativity scene and a Christmas tree, left. A few large candles in a safe position are also helpful. A reading desk or music-stand at the side with the narrator's book on it, as the narrator's parts are read, not recited. A doorway or gap in screens at the centre back is also a help.

Properties

Costumes for nativity scene, caps and aprons for cooks, a cap and bag for the postman
Christmas tree, with a sprig of mistletoe hidden by it
candles in holders
taper and matches
sledge piled with holly
tree decorations
posters (or a frieze) illustrating the Twelve Days of Christmas
a selection of Christmas cards
lantern, 2 collecting boxes, scarves and coats, for carol singers
boar's head and turkey, made of papier mache over chicken wire
Christmas cake with a crepe-paper ' frill '
half a dozen mince pies and a Christmas pudding
trays for food, covered in tinfoil

The music

Most of the carol tunes are familiar. ' Light the lamps and deck the fir tree' is sung to the Welsh tune ' New Year's Eve ', and ' While the silent world was sleeping ' to ' All through the night '.

All [*off stage or behind curtains*]

Christmas is coming, the goose is getting fat,
Please put a penny in the old man's hat.
If you haven't got a penny, a ha'penny will do.
If you haven't got a ha'penny, God bless you!

Narrator: As December comes around each year we prepare to celebrate the festival of Christmas—remembering the birth of Jesus Christ nearly two thousand years ago in Bethlehem. We try to show our love to others by presenting our families and friends with gifts and by giving to others who are less fortunate than ourselves. In schools and churches, on television and radio we see and hear nativity plays, carol services and Christmas programmes. Our homes are decorated with paper chains and greenery and coloured lights, while we enjoy ourselves eating foods which we only have at this season.

Why do we do these special things at this season and no other? This is what we are going to try to make clear in our acting, singing and dancing. But before we begin, we must realise that none of this would be taking place today but for something which happened that night so long ago—the birth of our Lord in the stable at Bethlehem.

[*All children except those in the Nativity tableau group themselves on the stage to sing the first verse of 'Once in Royal David's City', and remain on stage left.*]

Narrator: In many of our schools and churches we have cribs at Christmas-time. Sometimes we cut figures out of specially-made books to build up our scene. Sometimes we make models of the scene, using small dolls and toy animals. Very often we ourselves act the parts. This all helps to remind us of Jesus, our king, being born in a humble stable and having to sleep on the straw in a manger because there was no room for him at the inn. These scenes remind us of the people who visited the infant Christ, too; the shepherds and the wise men. But usually these scenes look very pretty and happy. The stable in Bethlehem would have been cold and dark and smelly, not at all the pretty picture we see in Christmas cards. When we remember that we are also reminded of all the people in the world today who have no proper homes, who live in terrible conditions, who are cold and hungry and need our help, not only at Christmas-time but all the year through.

Choir: [*while the Nativity scene players assemble and take their position in the tableau—right of stage*]
'O Little Town of Bethlehem', first two verses.

Choir *kneels, facing the tableau, to sing verse three:*
' O holy child of Bethlehem.'

[*Older members of Choir stand while younger children group themselves around the tableau and sing* ' Little Jesus, sweetly sleep.']

Narrator: Have you seen the lights on a Christmas tree? Christmas-time always makes us think of light. St John, in his gospel, tells us that Jesus was born as the light of the world. Have you looked up at the sky on a frosty night and seen the stars twinkling? The three kings who visited Jesus travelled many miles following a star. We remember all this in our Christmas decorations. Sometimes we make an Advent wreath with five candles in it. Four of them are red ones, and we light a new one on each of the four Sundays of Advent. In the centre of the wreath is a tall white candle which is lit on Christmas Day. This helps us to think of Jesus, the Light of God coming into the darkness of our world.

[*As the next carol is sung, one boy goes out for a taper to light some suitably-placed candles on the stage. If an artificial star could also be illuminated at this point, it would be most effective.*]

Choir: ' As with gladness men of old.'

[*During the singing of the last verse two boys go off to fetch the sledge with holly on it.*]

Narrator: We usually associate holly with Christmas, for this is the time when the holly tree stands out among the other trees. While most trees look like bare skeletons, the holly is green and glossy in December. Its bright red berries make it look gay—but the holly reminds us of the death of Jesus. The prickly leaves remind us of his crown of thorns and the berries of his blood. An old carol tells us of this.

Choir: ' The holly and the ivy.'

[*During the singing of this carol, two boys will bring in the sledge with the holly and lay sprigs of holly along the edge of the stage. During the last chorus, one child leaves to fetch a box of simple decorations which can be used quickly to decorate the tree, and another to be dressed as a postman.*]

Narrator: We always have a Christmas tree in our house. One legend tells us that a German saint called St Boniface discovered a tribe who had met beneath an oak tree to sacrifice a little boy to the cruel gods in whom they believed. The saint snatched away the little boy and chopped down the oak tree.

As it fell, he saw a little fir tree growing in its shadow. He turned to the pagan people and preached to them of Christ and then, pointing to the little fir tree, he told them that it was a sign of life which never dies, for it never lost its green colour. It came to a slender point which reached up towards the light and so it would be a sign of Christ to them. No longer were they to worship their wicked old gods, for the fir tree would always be a reminder to them of Jesus.

The baubles and tinsel with which we decorate our trees again remind us of light; so does the star at the top of the tree, which makes us think of the star which led the Wise Men from the east. Sometimes a doll is put on the top branch. We mistakenly call it 'the fairy on the Christmas tree'. What it really represents is not a fairy at all, but the angel who brought the news of the baby at Bethlehem to the shepherds on the first Christmas night.

[*Younger children skip around the tree while the older children decorate it. All join in singing 'Light the lamps and deck the fir tree'. Twelve of the smallest children skip off at the end of the dance to fetch posters for the Twelve Days of Christmas. Five go off to prepare for the cooks' scene, and two to get the carol singers' lantern and collecting-box.*]

Narrator: We enjoy opening our presents on Christmas morning and we enjoy giving presents to others. It is fun buying our gifts and wrapping them in gaily-patterned paper. It is even greater fun to watch others opening them and know that they are pleased. As we give these presents, let us remember the greatest gift that ever was, God's gift of his own Son. We can also remember the gifts of gold, frankincense and myrrh which the Wise Men brought to Bethlehem. How eagerly we wait for the postman each morning during the week before Christmas!

[*Loud knocking. One child enters dressed as a postman and gives a card to each child—these are placed along the edge of the stage with the holly. Each child can say a word of thanks or a Christmas greeting to the postman.*

As the next carol is sung, a child comes in during each new verse, carrying a poster illustrating that particular verse, so that a semi-circle is formed across the stage. If there is an acute shortage of children, two could unroll a frieze, a section at a time.]

Choir: 'The Twelve Days of Christmas.'

[*While the music is continued, the poster-bearers either file off, leave their posters and rejoin the choir or (preferably) hang the posters at pre-determined positions at the sides or back of the stage.*]

Narrator: We often find that hanging among our decorations is a sprig of mistletoe. Some people say that the ancient Druids who worshipped among the oak trees used the little white-berried plant as a symbol of love. Over the centuries the tradition grew of kissing under the mistletoe.

[*All join in the Mistletoe Dance. Two lines, one of boys, one of girls face each other and dance in groups of four. If there is a couple extra, they clap the rhythm until the second round when they will be drawn in and another couple will be standing.*

In fours: All join right hands in centre (right hand star)
Skip round for eight beats
All join in centre (left-hand star)
Skip round for eight beats
1st couple make arch—2nd couple under it
2nd couple make arch—1st couple under it
1st couple make arch—2nd couple under it
(The three arches must be made in a flowing movement occupying 12 beats.)
Form new sets of fours with new partners.

This is a progressive dance and as many rounds as wished can be danced. As the last round ends, a tall child should seize the piece of mistletoe from the Christmas tree and hold it over the couple at the front of the stage, who kiss each other on both cheeks. It is most effective if the two youngest do this.]

Music for the Mistletoe Dance

Narrator: Many of us join with the grown-ups on Christmas Eve and go from house to house singing carols. At the same time we make a collection for people in need, the sick or the homeless or those in distress. We have to wrap ourselves up warmly and we carry torches or lanterns so that we can see our music clearly.

[*One of the carol singers knocks.*
The door (real or mimed) is opened and the carol singers sing the first verse of either: 'Silent Night' or 'Ding Dong, Merrily on High'. After the carol:]

1st Child: That was lovely.

2nd Child: Do come right inside and sing another one.

3rd Child: Yes, come in—we'll all sing one together.

Choir: 'While the Silent World was Sleeping.'

1st Carol Singer: We are collecting for the homeless, to try to help them this Christmas. Would you like to give something?

[*All the children press forward towards the tin, which should have some money in it so that it will rattle when shaken.*
As the carol singers leave, the children call 'thank you' and Christmas greetings.]

Narrator: Christmas food is traditional, and while we are enjoying ourselves, mothers are busy preparing it. Sometimes, in the butcher's shop, we see a boar's head richly decorated. In the Middle Ages, pork was the meat traditionally eaten. By Christmas time, the pigs which had roamed in the great forests in the care of a swineherd, had grown fat on the acorns and beech nuts on which they fed. At the Christmas feast, a young page would carry the boar's head to the high table, where the lord of the manor and his lady sat, and this would be the signal for the feast to begin.

[*Enter one of the cooks, holding a tray with a large boar's head on it. He walks slowly and pompously to the front of the stage while the choir sings:*]

Choir: 'The Boar's Head Carol.'

Narrator: It was not until the time of Queen Elizabeth the First that turkeys were known here. They were brought back to this country from America, where they are still eaten on Thanksgiving Day. As they were such a very special dish, they came to be associated with the Christmas feast, the biggest of the year.

[*Enter second cook—holding a tray with a turkey on it. Joins first cook at the front of the stage.*]

Narrator: We love hot mince pies. Nowadays mincemeat is made of suet and many rich fruits, but originally it really was minced meat—minced mutton in a pastry case, which was oval to remind us of the shape of the manger in which Jesus slept. We also enjoy the rich cakes which we see decorated with icing and various wintry scenes.

[*Enter third and fourth cooks holding mince pies and a Christmas cake. They join the others.*]

Narrator: If we have any room left after our turkey, we eat our plum pudding. Just like the mince pies which are no longer made of minced meat, plum pudding is not made with plums, but originally it was made with prunes—which are, of course, dried plums.

[*Enter fifth cook carrying a plum pudding. He joins the other cooks. When all the cooks are on the stage, 'The Boar's Head Carol' is sung once more—and during it the cooks file out, led by the one carrying the boar's head.*]

Narrator: As we enjoy our Christmas food and fun, we must not forget the thousands of poor children who will have no food or gifts this Christmas. As we remember Jesus being born in a dark stable and being put to sleep in a rough manger, we must remember the refugees, the orphans and the homeless, and we must think how we can help them.

Choir: 'Away in a manger.'

Narrator: Children always look forward to a visit from someone else at Christmas time. He comes with his sledge and his reindeer and his sackful of lovely presents and fills our stockings to the top with good things. Who is he?

All: Father Christmas!

[*At this point, if the intention is to present gifts to the children, an adult member of the congregation or staff can walk from the back in costume and distribute the gifts. If this is not the case, one child dressed in costume can drag a sackful of boxes across the stage, waving to everyone, while the other children cheer.*]

Narrator: We all enjoy Christmas time. But as we enjoy it, let us never forget that it is a very holy time—a very special birthday, that of our Lord Jesus Christ. We shall not enjoy Christmas to the full if we do not join in the church, in school and in our homes to worship him. So let us all, here and now, children, parents and friends, stand and join together in singing to him.

All [*sing*]: 'O come, all ye faithful.'

[*At the end of the carol, those taking part in the tableau lead off immediately, while the music plays.*]

Narrator: There is now only one thing left to be said.

Choir: We wish you a Merry Christmas
We wish you a Merry Christmas
We wish you a Merry Christmas
And a Happy New Year.
Good tidings we bring
To you and your kin,
We wish you a Merry Christmas and a Happy New Year.

[*As this verse is sung for the second time the children lead off, waving to the audience.*]

A PLAY FOR ALL SEASONS

Mrs O. H. Plant, deputy headmistress of a church school in Bolton, wrote this nativity play, which shows all the seasons of the Church's year—and has parts for everybody

This play is designed for teachers who have been asked to present a nativity play in church or in school, and who perhaps prefer to work from a prepared script. It was originally done by our primary school as 'theatre in the round', and every child in the school took part in the play, but the numbers in the cast can be greatly varied according to your own circumstances. It lasts for about half an hour. Wherever possible, the audience should join in the carols. The children's verses can be accompanied by drums and recorders, or a piano can be used throughout.

[*The children of the choir enter to 'People look east, the time is near' (Oxford Book of Carols). They are led by garland bearers, who form an arch for them to walk through. The children carry holly, laurels, lanterns, garlands, a star on a long stick, a small Christmas tree; bowls, rolling-pins, jars of mincemeat; mops, brushes, dustpans. They group round the perimeter of the 'theatre', miming Christmas preparations. Among them is a mother with her family. As the music dies away, she speaks:*]

Mother: Let's sit down and rest. I'm getting so tired with all this Christmas rush.

1st child: I want Christmas to come quickly. It seems *such* a long time since last Christmas.

2nd child: What a lot has happened since then!

Mother: I'm glad you've made a scrapbook this year. Let's look at it now while we are resting.

[*As the mother turns the first pages of a large book, the choir sings, to the tune of 'I saw three ships':*]

Choir: Oh, what did January bring,
Bring to us all, bring to us all,
Oh, what did January bring?
Wise men were shown a baby King.

[*The three wise men appear with their attendants. They carry their gifts round the theatre and group at one end. Mother turns a page, as she does before every verse.*]

Choir: Oh, what did February bring,
Bring to us all, bring to us all,
Oh, what did February bring?
Sweet crispy pancakes and Lent began.

[*A group of children come in mixing batter and tossing pancakes. (If desired, they may be followed by another group carrying palm crosses, which may be put into a tray of ashes.) They join the first group (as do all the other groups in their turn.*]

Choir: Oh, what did stormy wild March bring,
Bring to us all, bring to us all,
Oh, what did stormy wild March bring?
St Patrick of Ireland, St David of Wales.

[*St Patrick should carry shamrock and his flag; St David carries a leek or daffodils. (If desired, the choir and the children could sing an Irish or Welsh carol.)*]

Choir: Oh, what did happy Easter bring,
Bring to us all, bring to us all,
Oh, what did happy Easter bring?
Jesus rose from the grave to be Christ our king.

[*A group of children mime any local Easter custom, such as rolling Easter eggs, or searching for eggs left by the Easter hare'.*]

Choir: Oh, what did showery April bring,
Bring to us all, bring to us all,
Oh, what did showery April bring?
St George fought the dragon who stood for sin.

[*This is a scene the children can dramatise freely.*]

Choir: And then came Holy Trinity,
Trinity, Trinity,
And then came Holy Trinity,
The three in one and one in three.
(*or* One living God in Persons three.)

[*St Patrick with his shamrock comes into the middle of the theatre and gives out some to the children.* (*If none is available, clover can usually still be found.*)]

Choir: Oh, Trinity lasted many a day,
Many a day, many a day.
Oh, Trinity lasted many a day—
Harvest time with September came.

[*A procession of harvest fruits and corn (real or symbolic) is carried and displayed at a suitable spot.*]

Choir: And what did golden October bring,
Bring to us all, bring to us all,
And what did golden October bring?
St Simon, St Jude and Hallowe'en.

[*If the two saints are the school's patrons, the children wear their school uniform; otherwise they carry emblems, a ship for St Simon, a Bible for St Jude. A second group follows carrying turnip lanterns, with a witch; they are followed by some saints—e.g. St Francis, St Christopher carrying a child, and St Giles carrying a banner marked 'All Saints' Day'.*]

Choir: And what did misty November bring,
Bring to us all, bring to us all?
And what did misty November bring?
St Andrew of Scotland, the fisherman.

[*St Andrew comes in with his net, fish and flag. (The children may here suggest miming the story where Jesus said 'Follow me', or a Scottish carol may be sung.)*]

Choir: And now Advent has just begun,
Just begun, just begun,
And now Advent has just begun—
The Angel tells Mary she'll have a son.

[*Mary is greeted by the Angel. As the music is repeated softly, the mother closes her book slowly, takes her children's hands and speaks:*]

Mother: And now it's Advent, the beginning of another year. Let's look at our Advent Calendar and light our first Advent candle.

[*The children at the back lift numbered cards to represent the windows in an Advent calendar, and count them off from* 1 *to* 24.]

Mother: When we open that window, we shall see baby Jesus in the stable. We must be ready for him. [*She lights the Advent candle.*] Let us be very quiet and say a little prayer. [*Her children lead the rest of the assembly.*]

[*The hymn 'The wise may bring their learning' (in 'Hear Us, Heavenly Father' (Oxford) and other collections) is sung here as a prayer, and is not announced.*]

[*While the hymn is sung, Mary walks away to join Joseph at the back of the hall* (*or out of sight*). *The choir join the other groups of children, only the child with card* 24 *remaining. The mother points to card* 24.]

Mother: Look! It's Christmas Eve. Let's put out the Christmas crib. Fetch the wooden stable. (*The boys who carried evergreens in the procession hold them out to form a roof.*) Bring the manger and the straw. (*One child bring in the manger; the straw comes from the harvest group.*) Fetch the shining star. (*The child who carries the star now goes behind the stable.*) Where is the little fir tree? (*The child with the Christmas tree brings it.*)

Children: Please tell the Christmas story again.

Mother: Listen carefully.

[*The choir sing 'Mary and Joseph'* (*Infant Music by Desmond MacMahon published by Nelson.*) (*If preferred, 'O little town of Bethlehem' may be hummed instead.*) *Joseph and Mary are seen. They approach the inn keeper, who shakes his head, but leads them to the stable and there stands well to the left. Angels close the entrance to the stable. One verse of 'While shepherds watched' is played. The shepherds come in, sit down, and pretend to be warming themselves round a fire.*]

Choir: 'The little fir tree' (*Child Education, 1967*) or 'While shepherds watched'. (*The angels part to show the interior of the stable.*)

Choir: '*Il est né, le divin Enfant*' (French Carol). (*Mary picks up Jesus*) 'Light the lamp, Joseph' or 'Away in a manger'.

[*The shepherds approach, and so do the Kings. A tableau is formed.*]

Finale: *The whole company sings 'Hark, hark, the Christmas bells'* (*Child Songs* by *Carey Bonner, NCEC*) *or some other favourite carol.*

This play calls for a good many properties and costumes, but these are very simple ones, most of which can be made by the children themselves. A complete list is as follows: Scrapbook; Advent ring with four candles; four long garlands; star on stick; manger; doll to represent the baby Jesus; small Christmas tree; articles to suggest preparation for Christmas (see first paragraph of play); 24 cards numbered clearly 1–24; frying pans with pancakes; Easter eggs; fisherman's net for St Andrew; shepherds' crooks; sheaf of corn, fruit and vegetables (real or artificial); lanterns; shamrock or clover in small basket; leek or artificial daffodils;

toy bird or animal for St Francis; white dresses for angels; blue dress and veil for Mary; brown tunics with cord belts for inn-keeper and saints; white tunic and plastic armour for St George; green tights, tunic and mask for the dragon; striped tunics and head coverings for shepherds; crowns, jewellery and bright tunics for the three kings; black shawl, skirt and witch's hat; 'All Saints' Day' banner.

The children will enjoy making their own properties, and often add their own ideas. For instance, our children made tonsures for the saints from old case balls. The costumes should present no great difficulty, apart from the dragon. We made our dragon from two old green curtains. First, two pieces were cut off to make arms. One curtain was made into a bag with a tapered end and a draw-string top; two slits were made horizontally to take the arms, and two slits were made vertically for the legs.

The child playing the dragon wore green tights and stepped into the bag, putting his legs through the leg slits. The second curtain, cut into strips with scalloped edges, made 'scales' over the first curtain. A cereal box cut along the middle of one larger side makes a good foundation for a mask, and pieces of egg cartons stuck on the top and sides suggest a scaly head.

To make the garlands, you will need two large cardboard rolls painted brown and fastened end to end with a piece of binding. Fresh evergreens are wired to the top and decorated with cones and red ribbons. Fir, rather than laurel or holly, in fact makes a fuller spray and forms a solid background for the crib. If a large foil star is fixed to a stick or tube painted black, it appears to hang in mid-air above the crib.

THE LITTLE WHITE INN

A Christmas mime for under-sevens by Mrs O. H. Plant

This service, with mime and carols, was written for an infant class in a Bolton primary school. The poem can be read either by one adult narrator or by several children, according to the number of those taking part. Characters in the order of their appearance are: the landlord and his wife; two merchants; two Roman soldiers with a prisoner; a family party of father, mother, two children and grandmother; Mary and Joseph; angels; shepherds; three kings.

The order of service	*The mime*
Narrator:	
Beside the gate at Bethlehem There stood a small and pleasant inn, And there the landlord and his wife Welcomed a crowd of strangers in.	Landlord and wife get ready to welcome customers
The merchants travelling from afar With spices, silks and scents for sale;	Merchants enter inn
Two Roman soldiers guarding fast A prisoner on his way to jail.	Soldiers march prisoner inside
Small children tugging mothers' skirts; Old people dragging aching feet; And fathers bracing weary limbs To haul their packs from some tired beast.	Cross mother and tired children, weary granny and father with pack enter and rest

Children sing carol: 'Hurry, little donkey.'

The order of service	*The mime*
Narrator:	
The travellers washed their dusty feet. Their hostess served them bread and wine, And for a treat she laid out plates Of dates, and grapes from her own vine.	All wash and eat, served by landlord and wife
The landlord rolled out mattresses; He filled a lamp and trimmed a wick. Two late arrivals caught his eye; He noticed one looked very sick.	Landlord mimes action in first two lines. Enter Joseph and Mary

The rooms were full; no beds were left!
How could he turn this girl away?
Then all at once an idea came—
He'd fill his stable with fresh hay.

Landlord indicates ' No room.' Has idea; indicates stable

Children sing carol: ' They came to Bethlehem.'

Narrator:

The landlord's wife was kind at heart
And brought a bowl of fresh goat's milk.
She grieved to see the look of pain
On the sweet face so soft, like silk.

Wife leads Mary to stable, makes her comfortable with Joseph's help, brings milk

She left some water close at hand
The sound of voices died away,
And Joseph wiped his young wife's brow.
The donkey gave one long last bray.

Wife leaves stable. Mary lies on floor, Joseph watches over her

All sing carol: ' O little town of Bethlehem.'

[*All remain seated to sing*]

Narrator:

The stars shone down on that white inn,
But one sent down a brighter ray. . . .
It seemed to grow until it flashed
Like lightning turning night to day.

And none in Bethlehem were awake
To see that wonder in the sky,
And none could hear the angel host
Above a new-born baby's cry.

Mary cradles baby in her arms

Children sing carol: ' The little fir tree.'

Narrator:

But high above on moorlands bleak
Some shepherds huddled round their fire.
Sometimes they joked; sometimes they dozed
Sometimes they talked of their Messiah.

Enter shepherds; they crouch round fire, rubbing hands. One falls asleep; others talk

When would he come, this mighty king,
And drive the legions back to Rome?
How could they guess that even now
He lived and breathed so near their home?

All sing carol: ' Once in royal David's city ', verses 1, 2, 5.

[*All remain seated to sing*]

Narrator:

And so it was that angels sang
And brought the news of Jesus' birth—
That God so loved us all, he'd given
His own son to the earth.

Angels appear to astonished shepherds

Children sing carol: ' On a lovely Christmas night.'

Narrator:

The proud young mother lifted up
The baby she had yearned to hold;
She took the sheepskin shepherds
brought
And wrapped him safe against the cold.

Shepherds go to stable, and give presents to baby

Children sing carol: ' Little Jesus, sweetly sleep.'

Narrator:

Along the rocky winding track
That led the way to Bethlehem's gate
Came wise men who had studied stars,
Who thought that stars were linked with
fate.

Enter kings, pointing to star

They came to seek a warrior king
Whose star foretold a mighty throne.
How could they know that Mary's son
Would only rule by love alone?

Kings come to stable and present gifts

Children sing carol: ' The Kings.'

Narrator:

A spider spun her silken web
Above the open stable door;
Two bright-eyed mice ran through a hole
And searched for grain amongst the straw.

The cock crowed twice out in the yard.
Some restless children left their bed
And playing hide-and-seek, one found
A baby in a manger bed.

The children in the inn wake up and creep out to play. One finds the stable, goes and fetches the others. Together they admire the baby

All sing carol: ' In the bleak midwinter.'

Narrator:

Under the early morning sun
The white stone inn still looked the same,
But the whole world was changed for all
The night our saviour Jesus came.

All in the inn wake up. The children rush in to fetch them. They all go to the stable and kneel before the baby

So let us thank God for his son;
Though we are selfish, poor and weak,
Yet here today we show our love,
And in our love his ways we seek.

Closing prayer

All sing carol: ' O come, all ye faithful ', verse 1 only. [*All stand to sing*]

Carols used in this service are as follows:

' Hurry, little donkey ' from *Songs of Spain*, by E. Barnard (Curwen)

' They came to Bethlehem ' from *Infant Music*, by D. Macmahon (Nelson)

' The little fir tree ' from the magazine *Child Education* (Evans)

' The kings ' from *Dunblane Praises, No. 2*

' On a lovely Christmas night ' from *Singing Fun*, by Wood and Scott (Harrap)

Other carols known to the children could, of course be substituted.

Ray Simpson employs a simple but lively blend of mime and choral speech in

DOWN TO EARTH

A Christmas project for older juniors or seniors with chorus, readers and mime. This may be done very simply with almost no props and few rehearsals or may be more elaborately produced. It is written for a performance in church, but can be adapted for use on stage. It was first performed by the Junior Church of St Andrew's Mission Church, Longton, Stoke-on-Trent.

If performed at the chancel, the chorus can sit in the choir stalls. They need to move out and back again after each action quickly and quietly.

Narrator: And God said, 'Let there be light'—but the people loved darkness rather than light.

[*The Narrator should make full use of dramatic pauses. As he speaks the Chorus crawls across the floor, their hands shielding their eyes, looking only at the floor. Chorus returns.*]

And God said, 'Let there be food for all.' But the hired labourers plundered God's vineyard for themselves.

[*As he speaks three fat people come from Chorus, laden with baskets of luxury foods, and munching; three thin persons sit cross-legged with empty rice bowls in their outstretched hands. Chorus returns.*]

And God said, 'Let there be love', but . . .

[*Chorus forms into three pairs or groups, one shooting, one hitting, and one turning his back on the other, chanting. . . .*]

Chorus: Hate, hate, hate . . . [*in rhythms of three. Chorus returns*].

Narrator: And so God said, as he looked out on his world: It's my world. I love my world. Will no one let me into my world? Old man there, will you hear?

[*Man sits or leans, no shoes, with pipe, reading paper.*]

Don't you know what's in the air?

Or widow woman there, will you stay in a rut, with your heart all shut, or will you let in the air?

[*Widow stands stiffly with hands clasped over heart, turning head aside from audience.*]

[*A student comes on, carrying a placard with ' anti everything ' written on it.*]

Student, your brain is alive, won't you look for a star to be your guide?

[*A current pop record starts, soft at first, gradually getting louder*]

Narrator: [*Gradual crescendo*]
Mother . . . master . . . priest . . . the poor . . . [*each steps out*].

[*Music stops in middle of next sentence, which is shouted.*]

Is there no one there who's pure?

[*There is a pause and a loud knocking from the Narrator. The characters leave together, and regroup into Chorus.*]

Chorus: Two, four, six, eight, who do we appreciate? M.E., M.E., M.E., Meee. Me, me, me. Me, me, me.
Give me more, more, more. Give me more, more, more.
Leave me alone, lone, lone. Leave me alone, lone, lone.
Me, me, me. [*Repeat*]
More, more more. [*Repeat*]
Alone, lone, lone. [*Repeat*]
Bingo!

[*This should be shouted, with hands outstretched, after a gradual crescendo. Immediately everyone disappears very quickly, or a spotlight is switched off or curtain drawn.*]

[*After a pause the notes of ' Blest are the pure in heart ' should be heard softly in the background. A girl (Mary) walks to the chancel steps and kneels.*]

Girl:
Lord, teach me that my heart may be
a little house that's fit for thee—
A house of shining window panes,
Clean from all smears and smuts and stains;
No blinds drawn darkly down, to hide
The things that lie and lurk inside,
And creep and mutter in the night;
For honesty is free as light.
So I will take my broom, and clear
Every dishonest thought and fear
And deed right out, that I may be
A little house that's fit for thee.

[*M. E. Proctor*]

O Lord my Saviour, every heart is open to you, no secret is hidden from you. Wash clean the thoughts of my heart; breathe in your Holy Spirit, that I may perfectly love with all my body and all my spirit. For you are my Maker, my Helper, my Redeemer and Friend, for ever. Amen.

Chorus: [*This could be sung solo or recorded*]

A humble, lowly, contrite heart,
Believing, true and clean,
Which neither death nor life can part
From him that dwells within.
A heart in every thought renewed,
And filled with love divine,
Perfect and right, and pure and good,
A copy, Lord, of thine.

[*Charles Wesley*]

Narrator: And so a teenage girl called Mary was chosen to give birth to a son.

[*Chorus returns to its place.*]

Chorus: *Sing* ' Little Donkey '.

[*Mary has been kneeling all this time. During the singing of ' Little Donkey ' she slowly walks to the back of the church, where she is joined by Joseph. Together they walk slowly back to the chancel step, arriving just as ' Little Donkey ' ends.*

They stand before the chancel step, which becomes blocked by the Chorus.]

Chorus: Two, four, six, eight, who do we appreciate? M.E., M.E., M.E. Meeeeeee.

[*The background chatter of* 'me, me' *continues quietly, as Mary and Joseph go to each member in turn with inquiring gestures, to be told by each one in turn. . . .*] No room.

[*After the last member has said ' No room ' the whole Chorus shouts ' No room ' repeatedly, with gestures signifying this. Mary and Joseph push through and walk up to the altar. They sit there. The Chorus returns to its place.*

A baby (*doll*) *may be seen with the couple at the altar, perhaps on straw on the top step, or Mary can mime holding the baby within a fold of her cloak.*]

Narrator: And so was born [*said very slowly*], in a smelly stable, the Son of Man; the Son—of God.

Chorus: No room, no room . . . [*whispered continuously as Narrator speaks*].

Narrator: This wondrous event, which was to change the way and the ways of the whole human race, was hid from the eyes of the millions, hell-bent on their selfish course. But it was revealed to those who were pure in heart. [*Chorus ceases. As each person is mentioned, he walks up to the Holy Family at the crib before the next person is named.*] A sheep farmer here. An office girl there. A teacher. A fireman, (etc.), who asked. . . .

All: [*i.e. all those at the altar. It may be more effective to have some or all of the Chorus remaining at the chancel, not joining in the singing.*]

What can I give him,
Poor as I am?
If I were a shepherd,
I would bring a lamb;
If I were a wise man
I would do my part:
Yet what I can I give him—
Give my heart.
[*Last verse of* 'In the bleak mid-winter'.]

Congregation, Chorus and **Readers** [*sing*]: 'Blest are the pure in heart.'
[*During the last verse all go out.*]

WHAT ON EARTH . . . ?

A nativity play with a difference for juniors, by Iona Wake-Walker

This play, which was based on an idea by Miss Jenny Ferguson, then St Alban's Diocesan Adviser, and performed in church, concerns two Space Children who land on Earth on Christmas Eve. They cannot understand all the lights and preparations, and they meet three children, who try to explain. First they see a shop, busy with the Christmas rush; then they see a home, with puddings being stirred and presents wrapped. Then they see a church being decorated, and hear about the coming of Jesus, and, as they still do not understand, the children show them a nativity scene being acted. Finally the Space Children begin to feel the message of hope for all, and prepare to return home to bring some light to their cold realms.

Cast

There are only five speaking parts. (At a pinch these could be cut to two: one Space Child and one earth child.) The various scenes can be rehearsed separately and co-ordinated by the speaking parts. We found it quite easy to have a plain table in the middle of the chancel, with actors carrying on the props which turned it into counter, kitchen table and then altar. We left it dressed as an altar and moved it back for the nativity scenes and the final prayers.

Clothes

Except for the nativity, for which most churches are used to providing clothes, the outfit for the Space Children was the only one to need special thought. We gave the boy white trousers and the girl a white skirt; both wore white shirts, chain belts, silver cardboard helmets from a toyshop, and gumboots with silver foil round the tops. Other characters were simply indicated: an apron for mother, a collar for the vicar, etc.

Properties

Shop scene: a red cloak, beard and sack for ' Father Christmas '; a few blown-up balloons; various toys.

Home: Silver Christmas tree, decorations, cards, pudding basin and spoon, stockings to hang up, parcels to tie, spectacles and knitting for Granny, and an (optional) reliable dog.

Church: Cross and candles, broom, dustpan and brush, vases and Christmas greenery, perhaps a piece of brass to polish.

Music can be provided by the organ or tape-recorded. A satisfying opening sound is needed for the arrival of the Space Children—perhaps a loud whistle followed by a roll on the thunder-sheet.

SCENE 1

[*The play opens with the voluntary, ' Lord of the Dance '. A loud rumble and a bang. Two Space-Children discovered sitting*]

Space Boy: Where are we?

Space Girl: You shouldn't have opened that door; it's soft here, luckily, or we might have been hurt.

SB: Do you think this can be Earth?

SG: Oh, how exciting! What are they doing over there with all those bright lights?

SB: People *do* live on Earth, then!
[*Enter three children.*]

Sandy: Hullo, who are you?

Pat: Why are you all dressed up?

SG: We come from Mars. Excuse me, but is this Earth?

Bobby: Yes, of course, but how did you get here?

SG: Fell! All his fault.

SB: It wasn't. Do you always have lovely lights and things?

Sandy: Not always; it's Christmas.

SB: Whatever is Christmas?

Pat: Don't you know what Christmas is?

Bobby: How can they? They probably don't have it up there.

Sandy: It's when Jesus was born.

SG: Who's he?

Sandy: Well, you know God?

SG: No; is that a sort of animal?

Sandy: Cor, no; God's the chap who made us. Well, not a chap, a sort of kind holy feeling who made us, and you, and shops, and . . . .

Pat: And houses, and trees and sea, and—oh, everything.

SG: I always thought there must be someone like that.

SB: Well, why do you have all the lights?
What are *they* doing?
[*Goes over to where the shop will be.*]
[*All go over to the side, and the shop becomes the centre scene.*]

SCENE 2

[*In a toy shop before opening time. Suggested speeches, to be divided up as seems best to Producer.*]

Now, we must have it gay for Christmas.
Put those balloons up there, please.
How much are these?
25 pence each—just right for filling stockings!
Now you are to dress up as Father Christmas, and here is your sack.
I love the children!
We shall soon have such a rush. . . .
I feel quite excited myself!
My feet will be killing me by Christmas Eve. . . .

[*Suggested actions: arranging toys; one person tries on a mask. Father Christmas put on his beard; a clockwork toy is wound up; a teddy bear growls, etc. Music throughout this scene is 'Jingle Bells', played in the background.*]

SCENE 3

[*Shop is cleared away behind children as they come into the centre again.*]

SB: Well, what are they so busy for?

Sandy: Because it's Christmas. Everybody gets excited.

Pat: You should see up home; all decorations and parcels.

SB and G: [*together*] Why?

Pat: Well, I suppose we're so glad God sent us Jesus, and we show it by giving each other presents.

Bobby: Have a look in here.

[*They go to the side again and the centre scene becomes the living-room of a house.*]

SCENE 4

[*Christmas preparations in a home. Father, mother, granny, assorted children, and perhaps a dog? Suggested actions: decorate room, hang up stockings, tie up presents, decorate Christmas tree: stir puddings, arrange cards, etc. Granny sits, knits, and directs operations.*]

SCENE 5

[*Children come to the front, as before.*]

SG: Well, they're going to have a good time!

SB: How did God send Jesus anyway—in a space ship?

Sandy: Oh, no; he's the most important part of all life, but God made him be born a man, a person like us, starting as a tiny baby.

SG: What's that huge place?

Pat: That's a church; that's a quiet place, because the quiet part of us is the bit that doesn't die. We go there to think about God.

Bobby: Come on in.

[*They 'go in' to the Church. This time it might be better if they sit in a pew to watch. The chorale 'Break forth, thou beauteous heavenly light'* (Bach) *begins and is played throughout the next scene.*]

SCENE 6

[*Inside a church being decorated for Christmas, a vicar and ladies are decorating, children helping. Suggested actions: children fetch water, people sweep up, clean brass, decorate tree, arrange greenery, put up candles.*]

SCENE 7

[*The children come up to the front again, and the church scene action gradually recedes.*]

SB: What did you mean about the bit of us that doesn't die? On Mars when people stop being alive it's all cold and dark and very sad.

Sandy: Oh no; Jesus showed us we go on living—the quiet part of us does, in some other way.

SG: Did people know Jesus was so important when he was born?

Pat: No, they didn't at all; he was only born in a smelly old stable!

Bobby: With no telly or anything.

Pat: And the baddies killed him in the end. But it didn't matter because his love wasn't killed and it goes on and on. He keeps coming, just like Christmas does.

SG: I think he does come to people on Mars too; there's something very shining about the good and kind people there.

Sandy: Look! They're just going to act the scene of Jesus being born; would you like to watch?

[*They sit down in their pew again.*]

SCENE 8

[*Nativity scene in mime, with perhaps Narrator reading Luke 2. 1–8, from New English Bible, and/or 'Away in a manger' quietly sung or played.*]

SCENE 9

[*Nativity scene remains as tableau. Children jump up and stand looking.*]

SG: I feel as though we are part of this, even though we live so many miles away. I know he made our Mars, too, and he knows everything about us.

SB: We must find our way back to Mars; we must tell them all this. I believe it will bring love and hope to our cold place, just as it does to the Earth.

Sandy: Wait! They're just going to say a prayer; will you wait and join in?

[*Turns to congregation.*]

Will you kneel, and join in too?

[*All the cast except the Nativity tableau come and kneel down at the chancel steps.*]

Priest or Leader: In the Name of the Father, and of the Son and of the Holy Ghost.

Father of us all, from the farthest star to the newest baby, we ask you to come among us and bless us today. Make us kind and loving, and help us to know you. We thank you for all your good gifts, and for homes filled with your love to give us all a happy Christmas. Amen. We ask you specially today to bless everyone who is sad, or ill, or lonely, or very old, and those who do not know you. Be with them, and help us to help them. Through Jesus Christ our Lord. Amen.

The Lord's Prayer.

All Sing: ' O come, all ye faithful.'

The Blessing.

IF CHRIST WERE BORN ON TEES-SIDE

A highly individual Christmas play, by some 8s to 11s, noted down by Ann Cooper

This play was first performed in a Middlesbrough church. It is not given here as an acting script, although many will certainly want to use it as a basis for ideas, but as an example of what sensitivity and ingenuity children can bring to working out in contemporary terms the essential truth of a Bible story. The play was made round three carols from *Faith, Folk and Nativity* (Galliard record also available). The first scene was based on the story printed on the inside back cover of *Faith, Folk and Nativity*. Mrs Cooper says: 'The children spoke the words themselves and I merely wrote them down in the hope that they might say roughly the same things at each rehearsal.'

[*All sing first verse of carol 'If Christ were born in Burnley'; for this play the town's name was changed to '* on Tees-side.']

[*Enter Gabriel and four angels.*]

1st angel: Isn't it awful, being born in a garage?

2nd angel: Yes, with all those earwigs and spiders—and germs.

Gabriel: Well, that's what he wants.

3rd angel: Well, all we can do is to get it really clean.

4th angel: Yes, we'll get it really spick and span.

[*All work hard.*]

1st angel [*finding newspaper*]: Listen to this. 'Peacemaker has his throat slit.' Isn't this a dreadful world!

2nd angel: Look what this says! There's a war on in Vietnam and one in the Middle East. Isn't it horrible?

3rd angel: I don't see why he wants to be born into this world.

4th angel: Why doesn't he wait another two thousand years and then it might be better?

Gabriel: I don't know, but he says he must be born tomorrow. Get on! [*He goes out while angels work on. Suddenly he rushes back.*] Stop! Put everything back as it was—the dirt, the germs, the lot!

All [*with great surprise*]: Why?

Gabriel: He wants to be born into the world as it really is.

[*All cast sing second verse of 'If Christ were born on Tees-side.'*]

[*Enter Joseph and Mary.*]

Joseph: It's no good, Mary. This house is condemned and I'm out of work. I'll never get a job here. We'll have to go back to Tees-side.

Mary: That's where you were born, isn't it?

Joseph: Yes. My father used to say there was plenty of work for joiners up there.

Mary: But what about the baby? Shouldn't we wait till he is born?

Joseph: No. I'm not having him come into a damp house that's falling down. We'll go as soon as I can get things organised.

[*They go out.*]

[*An inn yard. In the inn are the landlord, his wife and two barmaids.*]

Joseph: We'll try here, Mary. I never thought it would be so difficult to get a cheap room.

Mary: It looks rather expensive—and full.

Joseph [*knocking*]: Have you a room for us, please?

Landlady: No. We're quite full. It's this trade union conference.

Joseph: We must go somewhere out of this cold wind.

Mary: Haven't you a loft or cellar? We don't mind what it's like.

Landlady: I've told you. There's no room.

Landlord: Come on, Elsie. You're needed in the bar. Clear off, you two!

[*They turn away. The two young barmaids follow from the inn.*]

1st girl: Come with me. There's a garage over there where she lets her children play. I know it's empty.

2nd girl: It's quite warm and dry, and I think there's an old camp bed.

1st girl: When is your baby due?

Mary: Very soon. I didn't want to worry you, Joseph, but I think he will be born tonight.

1st girl: Oh! We must try and get you into one of the hospitals.

Mary: No. Please don't bother. I'm so tired—let us stay here. [*They go into garage. Short pause, then Mary sings 'Mary's View'.*]

[*In the inn. Trade union officials are drinking at the bar.*]

1st shop steward: We want more money, lads.

2nd S.S.: Get away, the more you get the more you want.

3rd S.S.: We want more time off and longer holidays.

4th S.S.: You're getting soft. We want *power*—the bosses out and the workers in. Strikes, that what we want. Hit 'em hard.

5th S.S.: I'm fed up with strikes. They do no good. They just cause trouble. They don't hurt anyone like the bosses, they hurt all the innocent people like kids and old people.

3rd S.S.: You don't know what you want. All I want is enough food to eat and a house to live and clothes to wear.

1st S.S.: We all want that. You've got to grab what you can while you can.

2nd S.S.: It's true, you can't trust anybody these days.

3rd S.S.: We need someone to show us the way. [*Enter angels.*]

Angels [*together*]: Glory to God in the highest and on earth peace, goodwill to all men.

2nd S.S.: Who are this lot?

Gabriel: See, where a child is born to you this night.

3rd S.S.: What do they mean? [*angels turn away.*]

5th S.S.: Let's follow them. I think this is important.

[*In the garage. Mary is sitting with the baby, Joseph standing behind. Enter 2nd, 3rd and 5th shop stewards with angels.*]

3rd S.S.: Oh, look, there *is* a baby. Isn't he canny? [*i.e. 'lovely'.*]

2nd S.S. [*scornfully*]: Is this our leader?

5th S.S. [*dropping to his knees*]: This is the Saviour of the world! [*Outside the inn. Enter a Russian, an Indian and an American. They knock at the inn door. Landlady and 1st Girl come out.*]

American: Is this the place where the child is born?

Landlady: I don't know anything about a child.

Girl: I do. Come on. Over here. [*She takes the three to the garage.*]

2nd S.S.: Who are these?

Russian: We are from the United Nations. I am from Russia.

American: And I'm an American.

Indian: And I come from India.

3rd S.S.: How did you get here?

Russian: We were on our way to New York from Geneva when the plane was hi-jacked by those angels over there. When we landed they vanished and we found we were at Tees-side airport. They had told us to find the child born in the garage for he would solve the problems of the world. [*All sing " Where is he?" the wise men asking.' Visitors present gifts. Enter landlady.*]

Landlady: I'm sorry I was so cross. Here's a shawl for your baby. As soon as these people have gone you can come into the house.

Mary: I never thought today would end so happily!

[*All sing last verse of ' If Christ were born on Tees-side'.*]

Gabriel: But what they forget is that he is born somewhere every day.

THE 'ZITHER CAROL' MIME

M. E. Curtis describes a simple service given by the children of Holy Trinity, Cirencester

Our Sunday school had only been going three months when Christmas came round. Nevertheless, we wanted to take a part in the Christmas celebrations. As a first venture, it was decided to hold a Carol Service with readings and a Nativity tableau.

As there was no time to prepare an elaborate presentation, and our only rehearsal time was during Sunday school sessions, we avoided speaking parts and chose simple costumes and a minimum of props, e.g. a wooden box camouflaged with straw for the crib, and a wooden stool as a seat for Mary.

Costumes

Mary: dark blue headdress which covered shoulders, over a skirt made from a piece of sheet.

Joseph: long coat (dressing gown), striped headscarf, wooden staff.

Shepherds: cloaks made from sacks, head squares, wooden crooks. (One boy brought a real shepherd's crook.)

Angels: surplices over pieces of sheeting for ankle-length skirts. Circlets on heads, made from stiff paper covered with foil.

Kings: crowns made from carboard covered with gold foil. (Glued-on 'clear gums' make good jewels.) Cloaks from colourful material. Gold: a brass box. Frankincense: a small metal bowl. Myrrh: a small bath salts jar, covered with coloured foil wrappings from chocolates.

The tableau was built up as the Christmas story unfolded in the readings and carols, and was staged on the raised step leading to the chancel. Each age-group in the school provided two or more performers for the tableau, the readers and choir coming from the older groups.

The Service opened with a carol for the congregation: 'O come, all ye faithful'.

Reading [*from the pulpit*]: St Luke 2. 1–7.

Carol: 'Once in royal David's city', verses 1 and 2 only, sung by the choir. [*During the singing, Mary and Joseph entered, Mary placed the baby in the crib and sat beside it. Joseph stood by her side.*]

Carol: 'Zither Carol' [*a Czech folk-tune arranged by Sir Malcolm Sargent and published as sheet music by the Oxford University Press, also in 'Carol, Gaily Carol' (A & C. Black)*]

Verse 1: *Three small children entered, bringing their toys which they placed by the crib, and remained kneeling.*

Verse 2: *Three angels entered and stood behind the crib.*

Reading: St Luke 2.8–17.

Verse 3 of '*Zither Carol*': *Shepherds, led by an angel, took up position round crib.*

Reading: St Matthew 2. 1–12.

Verse 4: *The kings entered, presented gifts and took up pre-arranged positions to complete the tableau.*

Verse 5: *Sung with tableau in position.*

After the tableau dispersed, one of our young teachers sang two carols with guitar accompaniment: 'Little Donkey' and 'Mary's Boy Child'.

We concluded with two carols for the congregation: 'Away in a manger' and 'O little town of Bethlehem'.

A cordial invitation was given to parents and others interested in our work with the children to come to this service, and it was most gratifying and encouraging that so many did so. The opportunity was taken to give a brief explanation of the aims and work of the Sunday school, following modern methods of teaching based on *Alive in God's World.* Parents were able to see some of the children's work—both their individual and collective pictures, models, etc.—as this was on display at the back of the church for the service.

HOW FAR IS IT TO BETHLEHEM?

A festival devised by David Hastings for a primary school in Salisbury, which can be adapted for smaller groups

'What are we going to do this Christmas?' This must be a question that faces us every year, and each year, no doubt, we rack our brains how we are going to present the eternal truth of God Incarnate to our children, to their parents and to those who attend our annual carol services and nativity plays in church or in school.

I too was faced with this question. How *do* we present the Christmas story in an interesting and lively way without repeating the well-worn 'set tableaux' or Carols and Nine Lessons, and yet at the same time keep the spirit of Christ coming to earth as a human being?

Having grappled with the thought for some months, I did some research. In my reading I discovered how Christmas is celebrated in different parts of the world, and tried to amass a store of information about customs of welcoming the Christ-Child, and to discover particularly how children are involved in the festivities.

I was fascinated by what I found. I learnt a great deal that was new and gradually began to see a new way of presenting Christ in Bethlehem. I wrote notes, edited them, and so 'How far is it to Bethlehem?' was conceived and born.

Having prepared a draft script, I then had to sort out how to involve as many children in school as possible, from the very youngest to the oldest. By careful planning we were able to involve almost every child in the school, a total of some 300 infants and juniors. But the basic idea lends itself to adaptation, and by reducing the characters, doubling parts and omitting sections as necessary, this could be given by quite a small day or voluntary school.

After an initial briefing session on the script, the children with their teachers began rehearsing in class units. Props were kept to a minimum and made by the children. Simple costumes were made by parents and children.

The choir had the main task of helping weld the theme together, and much enjoyed learning carols from other countries and watching the words, action and music festival blend together.

Rehearsals were kept to a minimum. We had about five in the church. Timing was relatively easy because we sat all the cast in the side aisles of the church, and they just came out of their places at their cue. They performed the tableaux on a portable stage which we borrowed for the occasion from our Diocesan Religious Drama Fellowship; its blocks are three feet high, which allowed the children to be seen from all parts of the church. We sat the choir on the back part of the stage and in the chancel to form a backcloth to the action. They all dressed in national costumes, to add colour to the scenes.

The children had no speaking parts, but took their cues from the Narrator (a member of the staff) and the music. This helped to give the festival flow and movement.

It all proved a great success with the parents and friends of the school; we had a packed church and some people had to stand at the back! We all felt very encouraged by this response, and from all accounts it would seem that people appreciated this different presentation of the Christmas theme. One could not try to repeat such a service every year, and so we hope to do one of this kind every two years, alternating with a more traditional service of readings and carols.

In all this we realise that we can, with thought and preparation, make ready for Christ's coming at Christmas. In no way do we lose the vision of 'The Word made flesh' Indeed, it is true to say that we became more aware of Christ's coming to us in Bethlehem.

THE PROLOGUE

Narrator: At the very beginning of all things God made the universe we know. The earth lay empty and dead darkness blacked out the deep seas, great winds lashed the water.
'Let there be Light!'
and the world was filled with light.

Music: [*Procession of Sun, Stars and Moon to central stage area.*]

Narrator: The Sun, the Moon and the Stars.
These are our guides by day and night.

Carol: 'Can you count the stars that twinkle?'
[*During this the Sun, Moon and Stars exit. One star is left on stage.*]

Narrator: One star remains, for this one is to be our guide tonight as we make our journey across the world.

Carol: ' Every star shall sing a carol ' [*first verse only—during which the Star exists.*]

SEQUENCE 1: THE ANNUNCIATION

[*While the Narrator reads, the scene is enacted in mime.*]

Narrator: God sent the Angel Gabriel to a town in Galilee called Nazareth. He had a message for a girl promised in marriage to a man named Joseph. The girl's name was Mary.
The angel came to her and said, ' Peace be with you! The Lord is with you and has greatly blessed you!' Mary was deeply troubled by the Angel's message, and she wondered what his words meant.
The Angel said to her: 'Don't be afraid, Mary, for God has been gracious to you. You will become pregnant and give birth to a son and you will name him Jesus.'
Mary said to the Angel, ' How can this be? '
The Angel answered, 'The Holy Spirit will come on you, and God's power will rest upon you. For this reason the Holy Child will be called the Son of God.'
' I am the Lord's servant,' said Mary. ' May it happen to me as you have said.'
And then the Angel left her.

Carol: ' The Angel Gabriel from heaven came ' (verses 1–3).

SEQUENCE 2: THE JOURNEY BEGINS

Carol: ' How far is it to Bethlehem? ' (verses 1–4).

Narrator: Christmas!

Everywhere people are getting ready for Christmas. Behind closed doors children are planning surprises. Delicious things are cooking in the kitchen. Houses and churches trimmed with green boughs. Candles are lit. Eyes shine. People sing. The days are cold. The nights are long. But the air is full of magic and bright with love.
Around the world, Christian children are waiting impatiently to celebrate the birthday of Jesus.

Carol: ' People, look East ' (verse 1).

[*During this music the Bethlehem Star comes on to stage.*]

SEQUENCE 3: FRANCE

Narrator: Our Christmas star leads us to the first stop of our journey.

To France, where people go to Midnight Mass and then celebrate the coming of the Christ Child by meeting for an elaborate Christmas supper, and no doubt, for some music with fife and drum.

Carol: 'The Little Drummer Boy.'

SEQUENCE 4: GERMANY

Narrator: Most of us have a Christmas tree in our homes. Our star leads us now to Germany where we see a group of children preparing their tree.

[*Children enter, bringing a Christmas tree with them, which they decorate. As they do so*—]

Narrator: One legend tells us of a German saint called Boniface, who met a tribe beneath an oak tree. They were about to sacrifice a little boy to the cruel gods in whom they believed. The saint snatched the boy away and chopped the oak tree down. As it fell, he saw a fir tree in its shadow.

Boniface then pointed to the fir tree and said that it was a sign of life which never dies, for it never loses its green colour. It comes to a slender point reaching towards the light, and so it would be a sign of Christ to them.

Carol: ' O Tannenbaum.'

Narrator: Our children from Germany now follow the star on its journey to the crib.

Carol: [*as children exit*]:' Ihr Kinderlein kommet' (verses 1 and 2].

SEQUENCE 5: SWEDEN

Narrator: To Sweden now, where Christmas celebrations begin on 13th December—St Lucia's Day—and it is a custom that the oldest girl in the family is the Lucia Bride. Dressed in a white robe with a red sash, and wearing a crown of greenery and lighted candles, she wakens the family by singing ' Santa Lucia ' and gives each member breakfast of coffee and saffron cakes.

Carol: ' Now St Lucia's Day is come.'

[*During this, we see the St Lucia Bride, and her family being awakened.*]

SEQUENCE 6: HOLLAND

[*The Star is once more on stage and a group of children await arrival of St Nicholas.*]

Narrator: In Holland everybody joins in celebrating the birthday of St Nicholas on 5th December. Before 5th December St Nicholas, or Sinterklaas, as Dutch children like to call him, is supposed to come sailing into Amsterdam on a big ship from Spain. He brings with him a great white horse and his faithful companion, Black Peter [*Enter St Nicholas and Black Peter through church*].

They ride through the streets and are greeted by crowds of cheering children. After the procession is over St Nicholas and Black Peter have a big job to do delivering presents to everybody in the whole country.

Carol: 'Let joy your carols fill.'

SEQUENCE 7: SWITZERLAND

Narrator: Our star now leads us on our journey to the snowy mountains of Switzerland. Here boys and girls eagerly await the arrival of the Swiss St Nicholas between the 4th and 6th of December. Let us pause for a while as we hear a Swiss lullaby for Christmas time.

Carol: 'Little Michael's Carol.'

SEQUENCE 8: POLAND

Narrator: In Poland the Festival of the Star is celebrated as soon as the first star in the sky appears. All that day children and grown-ups eat nothing until evening comes and it is time for the festive Christmas Eve Supper. As soon as the children spy the first star, they rush to tell their mother.

[*This is mimed as Narrator speaks.*]

At midnight, according to tradition, church bells ring, calling all Polish families to come to the Pasterka, the Shepherd's Mass. The brightly lighted church is decorated with Christmas trees and a crèche (or manger) has a place of honour until 6th January.

Music: 'Infant Holy' [*during which a procession of Nativity figures bearing candles appears to form a tableau, watched by the family from the mime.*]

SEQUENCE 9: CANADA

Narrator: Our star now leads us from the European continent to the American continent, where Christmas is celebrated in a multitude of ways.
We see first a group of Huron Indians from Canada as they celebrate the coming of the Christ Child.

Music: 'T'was in the noon of wintertime.'
[*Red Indians enter from various parts of church to form tableau in wigwam shapes.*]

SEQUENCE 10: AMERICA

Narrator: From the land of the Indians we pass on to the land of the cowboys, to the wide-open spaces of the prairie lands.

Carol: 'The Cowboy Carol.'
[*Group of cowboys 'ride' on to the music, and form tableau on stage*]

SEQUENCE 11: GREAT BRITAIN

[*Enter carol-singing party, singing 'The Holly and the Ivy'. They form tableau, and sing 'We wish you a Merry Christmas'.*]

Narrator: A familar part of Christmas in this city and all over our land at this time of the year. And why do they do it? Is it not to remind us of the true meaning of Christmas? How far is it to Bethlehem?
Let us now prepare ourselves for the final part of our journey—the Star now leads us to Bethlehem and a reminder of God's love in sending Jesus Christ to earth.

Music: 'Come ye now at Christmas to Bethlehem.'

SEQUENCE 12: BETHLEHEM

[*Mary and Joseph walk slowly up central aisle as Narrator speaks.*]

Narrator: When it was nearly time for Mary's child to be born, a law was announced by Augustus Caesar that all the people in the country should be registered and everybody had to go to the town where they had been born for this registration to take place. Joseph and Mary went from Nazareth to Bethlehem. Although they looked everywhere for a room to stay, the town was full, so they had to sleep in a stable. Here Mary's baby was born, and she wrapped him up and laid him in a manger.

Carol: 'The Farmyard Carol'

SEQUENCE 13

Narrator: Not far away there were some shepherds. An angel appeared to them telling them of Christ's birth, and they hurried off and found Mary, and Joseph, and saw the Baby lying in the manger. Later three Wise Men, or Kings, by tradition named Caspar, Melchior and Balthazar, came to see the Child, and to present their solemn gifts with strange and special meanings: gold for his kingship, frankincense for his priesthood and myrrh for his death.

Music: 'The Grasmere Carol.'

[*During this carol the shepherds and Wise Men process through church to form a final tableau of Bethlehem.*]

SEQUENCE 14

Narrator: So now our journey is complete. All roads have come to Bethlehem. We have brought an offering of this festival to God's own son. And that is what Christmas is all about: a child coming to earth, to grow into a man who would live and die and rise again for us. . . . God's gift to us all at Christmas.
'In the beginning was the Word,
and the Word was with God, and the Word was God.
And the Word was made flesh, and dwelt among us,
and we beheld his glory, the glory as of the only-begotten of the Father, full of grace and truth.'

Carol [*sung by all*]: 'O come, all ye faithful.'

[*During this carol a final procession of representatives of each country come to the crib. After this the Nativity tableau processes out through the church to leave an empty stage.*]

NOW ST LUCIA'S DAY IS COME

(*Tune:* Good King Wenceslas)

1. Now St Lucia's day is come,
Darkness cannot linger.
Cold, soon conquered by the sun,
Lifts his icy finger.

Chorus: Christ will come to be our light,
Laid within a manger.
Fiend of Hell, now vanquished quite,
Cease to be our danger.

2. Through the village let us go
Light and plenty bringing,
Man and beast awaken too,
Hearken to our singing.

Chorus: Christ will come, etc.

3. Village, farmhouse, cot and byre
Rouse we with our chanting:
Blessings bring with candles' fire;
Naught this year be wanting!

Chorus: Christ will come, etc.

Carols used in this festival are as follows:—

'Ihr Kinderlein kommet' ('O come, little children'). *Carols of the Nations,* Compiled and arranged by Ruth Heller (Blandford Press, 62½p). ('O Tannenbaum' is in the same book).

'Let joy your carols fill'. Words by Frank Fletcher, Dutch tune arr. Leslie Russell, *Oxford Choral Songs* (O.U.P., W50. 2½p).

Little Michael's Carol. Swiss Carol arr. by Desmond MacMahon (*Elkin Choral Series,* 2278. 6½p).

Carol of the Huron Indians ('Twas in the Moon of Wintertime'). Arr. Ralph Hunter (Curwen, 72639. 5p).

'Come ye now at Christmas to Bethlehem.' *Mortimer Series of Choral Music,* No. 656 (Ascherberg, Hopwood and Crew Ltd. 5p.)

The Farmyard Carol. To be found in *Eight Songs to sing about Christmas* by Mark Hankey, 20th Century Light Music Group. (Josef Weinberger Ltd. 35p).

The Grasmere Carol. Words and music by Arthur Somervell (*Novello,* E.A. 164. 9p.)

The Cowboy Carol. Words and music to be found in *A Cowboy Christmas* (Blandford. 10p).

An original, touching play for Epiphany by Rosalie K. Fry

REST ON THE FLIGHT

Characters

Zachary, Hannah, Ruth, Bedouin children.
Three Kings.
Joseph.
Mary.

Scene

A small fire smoulders in front of a Bedouin tent in the wilderness. Low rocks rise behind. Single brilliant star in sky at back.

[*Zachary crawls out of tent, leaps to his feet and swings round eagerly towards the star, then bounds up rocks towards it and stands gazing.*]

Ruth [*inside tent*]: Is it still there, Zachary?

Zachary: Yes, indeed, and shining just as brightly as ever.

[*Ruth crawls out of tent and stands gazing too.*]

Ruth: I do wish our father were not away just now. He might have been able to tell us what it means. I am so afraid it may have vanished before he comes home again.

[*While she is speaking her older sister Hannah opens flap of tent and comes out, carrying cooking pot. She also pauses to look up at star.*]

Zachary: Perhaps it has come to foretell some tremendous battle—that would be exciting.

Hannah: Oh no, not war—it is far too beautiful to tell of war.

Ruth: I am sure it must be something very wonderful and good.

Hannah: Come now and eat. [*Puts cooking pot on hearth.*] And you might fetch more firewood, Zachary, it's cold out here in the wilderness before the sun comes up.

[*Zachary fetches wood, then Hannah hands each a wooden spoon and the three sit down, dipping their spoons into the communal bowl in turns. Suddenly Zachary swings round and listens, spoon raised.*]

Zachary: Listen! I hear camel bells and a thud-thud-thud that sounds like many camels trotting over stony ground. [*Jumps up and runs to look off-stage.*] It is, too, a whole cavalcade, coming this way.

Hannah: But who would come out here? Our tent is far from any caravan route.

Zachary [*excitedly*]: They're coming anyway. They look like kings, three splendid kings in jewelled robes with a whole retinue of servants.

Ruth [*cowering fearfully beside the fire*]: If we keep quite still they might pass by and never notice us.

Zachary: They're getting off their camels now. They must have seen our fire.

[*Enter Three Kings. Zachary bows while the girls jump to their feet and Ruth runs to the protective shelter of Hannah's arms.*

1st King [*turning disappointedly to his two companions*]: Nothing but children, Bedouin children. What interest could our news be to these? [*Then, to Zachary.*] Are there more of you? Your parents?

Zachary: Our father is away and will not return until the moon is in the second quarter.

Hannah: And our mother is dead these many years.

2nd King: I see no reason why we should not tell our news to children as well as to their elders.

3rd King: Particularly since our tidings concern a child.

Zachary: Tidings? What tidings?

Ruth: Is it about the star?

1st King: Ah, so you have wondered about the star and what it foretells? [*Children nod, drawing closer.*]

1st King: We have studied the ancient Scriptures and have discovered that this star foretells the birth of a King—

2nd King: The Son of God.

3rd King: And King of Heaven.

1st King: So we went in search of him and followed his star until we found him, the mighty King of Heaven, the little Son of God.

Zachary [*disappointedly*]: Little? Is this mighty King just a small man, then?

2nd King: The mighty King is a baby in his mother's arms.

Zachary: A baby . . . you came so far and you only found a baby?

1st King: We came so far and we found the one we came to see.

2nd King: We all bowed down and worshipped him and gave him our prophetic gifts of gold and frankincense and myrrh, signifying power and beauty and sorrow as foretold in the Scriptures.

3rd King [*sadly*]: And now this long-foreshadowed sorrow threatens to touch him first of all, for Herod the king is anxious that the child be put to death.

Children: A *baby* . . . put to death?

1st King: That is Herod's wish. But perhaps the child's guardians will be warned, even as we ourselves were warned.

Zachary [*curiously*]: How were you warned?

2nd King: God told us in a dream that we should not return to Herod, and so we are travelling back to our country by another route.

1st King: But come now, our camels are fed and watered and we must continue on our journey and carry the tidings to our own people.

Hannah: But first may we offer you hospitality and what simple food we have?

1st King: It is a kindly offer, child, but our camels carry all the wine and food we need, and we must be on our way. We have many leagues to travel before nightfall.

[*Exeunt Kings. The children watch them out of sight, then the girls return to sit by the fire while Zachary paces restlessly to and fro.*]

Zachary: To think that the Son of God is a helpless baby in danger of death! I wish I were old enough to swing a sword and fight for him myself—I'd soon kill old Herod!

Ruth [*softly*]: I wish I could give him the things a little baby needs.

Zachary: We had nothing to give those earthly kings. What have we to offer the King of Heaven?

Ruth: We have a beautiful fire to keep him warm, and fresh goat's milk for him to drink, and clear spring water in which to wash his face and hands.

Hannah: And loving hearts and a peaceful home, which surely are the greatest needs of all.

[*Zachary settles down beside his sisters and all gaze into the fire.*]

Ruth: And I would dearly love to sing him a lullaby to soothe him off to sleep.

[*Ruth starts to sing a lullaby and the others join in. After the final verse they hum the melody through once more, gently rocking as they sing. Zachary suddenly lifts his head.*]

Zachary: Someone else is coming! [*Goes to look off-stage.*]

Ruth: More Kings?

Zachary: No indeed, just an ordinary couple this time, the woman riding on a shabby little ass.

[*Joseph enters, leading Mary, her cloak draped around the baby cradled in her arms.*]

Joseph: We saw your fire. We are cold and weary. May we come and rest awhile?

Zachary: Why, yes, indeed, and welcome. [*Draws forward a seat for Mary.*]

Joseph: We are escaping into Egypt from King Herod's soldiers.

Zachary: Egypt? That is a long way to be travelling. [*Glances doubtfully at Mary.*]

Joseph: Aye, a long, weary journey and full of dangers.

Zachary: I wlll fetch water to bathe your poor tired feet and a bundle of hay for the little ass.

Hannah: And I will warm some goat's milk over the fire. [*Kneels, holding pannikin over flames.*]

[*Ruth sidles close to Mary and peeps inside the cloak.*]

Ruth [*wonderingly*]: A baby . . . [*looks up at Mary*]. Is he . . . is he the little King of Heaven?

[*Mary smiles and nods. Zachary returns with a pitcher and sits down beside Hannah on the hearth.*]

Ruth: Perhaps he would like a little lullaby?

[*Ruth kneels beside Mary who puts an arm about her as she

begins to sing. Lights dim, and the other two children begin to nod drowsily. Ruth sings the final verses in darkness, then lights come on again gradually. Joseph rises. Mary pauses to settle the sleeping Ruth gently against the seat, then she and Joseph walk slowly off stage. It grows lighter. The children wake and look, bewildered, then get slowly to their feet.]

Zachary: They've gone!

Ruth: But we didn't dream them, we didn't, we didn't!
[*Zachary runs out and quickly returns.*]

Zachary: The ass has gone too, and all the hay I gave him. But he was here all right, his little hoofmarks are plain to see around the spring.

Hannah [*slowly*]: The water has gone from the pitcher. . . . .

Ruth: And the pannikin is empty too, every drop of the milk is gone, look! [*Turns pannikin upside down. Then, with a sudden smile.*] So we really did give him the things he needed on his flight—

Zachary [*thoughtfully*]: You're right. We weren't able to fight for him, but we could give him food and warmth.

Hannah: And comfort and rest on the journey.

Ruth: And love . . . and a little spell of peace to carry with him into the future, whatever it may hold.

THE TWELVE REPORTERS

by T. H. Ashcroft and D. H. Hedley, is the first of three short plays for juniors, which could be used in church or during Assembly

[*The twelve reporters, each with a large card or banner inscribed with the first letter of his surname, are spaced in random order about the hall or church. Each indicates his letter as he gives his name. (Girls could include a Christian name.) They speak in turn, as follows.*]

Trevor: My name is Trevor—' T ' for Trevor. [*He holds his card forward.*] I am a reporter for PHT. In case you don't know, PHT stands for the words PAST HISTORY TELEVISION. Today (or ' yesterday ', if you prefer it that way), I am speaking from Nazareth. We now see many people leaving the town because of an order given by the current Roman Emperor. Everybody is to be counted at the place of his birth—and it is proving highly inconvenient.

Harrison: My name is Harrison—' H ' for Harrison. We've got our cameras fixed by the River Jordan. These people you see are following the river down to Jericho. They're going this way because they don't want to travel through Samaritan country. Quite a colourful sight: with the little trotting donkeys and caravans of camels.

Robinson: My name is Anne Robinson of PHT. I am based at Jericho and I have just spoken to one of the travellers, who has come into the city. That's his young wife riding by on the small donkey. Looks rather tired, doesn't she?

Ibbotson: My name is Ibbotson. I am stationed half-way up the long, steep road that leads to Jerusalem and Bethlehem. Here's a straggling line of people coming up the dusty road and they all seem weary. No wonder—they are going to pay their taxes!

Simpson: My name is Simpson. It's very cold where I stand. I'm on one of the hills overlooking Bethlehem. Had quite a job getting the cameras up here—but it's worth it for the grand view. Look at the shepherds and the sheep. And, what's that . . . Hello—where are those three shepherds off to?

Carroll: I am Carroll—' C ' for Carroll. Here I am in the middle of Bethlehem. Oh, what a crowd. Just look at the pushing and jostling. I can hardly move for donkeys and camels!

Smith: My name is Smith of Past History Television. There are thousands of people here in Bethlehem tonight. I've no idea where some of them will sleep. Hey, you—mind that cable!

Ingram: My name is Susie Ingram—' I ' for Ingram. Look at this crowd—it's growing every minute. I've been talking to a man and woman, who have just come in all the way from Nazareth. He's trying to find a place where they can put up for the night. Good luck to them!

Noel: My name is Noel. I am standing outside this crowded inn. Look at the innkeeper at the door—so busy he's going mad! Says he's even got two people bedding down in his stable!

Owen: My name is Owen PHT. Did you see those three shepherds rushing past? One of them said something about a star and a stable. Heaven only knows what he meant!

Rafferty: I am Rafferty—' R ' for Rafferty. It's a lovely night here above Bethlehem. I say: just look at those stars—especially that big one. Nobody has ever seen a sky like this before!

Brown: My name is Brown—reporter with PHT. I've just come out of this little stable you see here. There's a donkey inside and some cows. I saw a man and a woman—and three kneeling shepherds, too. But the thing that really caught my eye was an old, broken manger with a baby in it. You'll not believe me, but the stable looked like a palace with that little chap lying there. Pity we couldn't get our cameras in—but the place was too small. . . . I wonder who the baby is?

[*The twelve reporters now close up into a straight, compact line, with the letters in their correct order and space beween the words: ' Christ is Born '.*]

THE CHRISTMAS BELLMAN

by T. H. Ashcroft and D. H. Hedley

Cast

Riot	later	**Peace**
Greedy	,,	**Helpfulness**
Pride	,,	**Modesty**
Hate	,,	**Love**
Jangle	,,	**Serenity**
Trouble	,,	**Happiness**
Noise	,,	**Quietness**
Discord	,,	**Harmony**

The Bellman

[*One by one, the first eight characters appear. Each has a card, inscribed on both sides with names as given above. They first display the names on the left.*]

Riot: My name is Riot, as you can see by my—er—visiting card. I love Trouble. My favourite hobby is knocking the helmet off a copper! You'll have seen me often on TV. I'd like to start something here!

[*Enter Greedy.*]

Who are you?

Greedy: Greedy's the name and greedy's the nature. I don't care what happens to anybody else—so long as I get plenty.

[*Enter Pride.*]

Hello—who's this?

Pride: My name is Pride. The peacock has nothing on me. Excuse my keeping my nose in the air. I just can't help it.

Riot: I'll excuse anything if you can sniff out Trouble with that big nose of yours. Stand by our Greedy Piggie—you'll like his sty—er—style!

[*Enter Hate.*]

And who are you?

Hate: They call me Hate. And I call myself Hate. I hate everybody—except myself, of course.

Riot: We shall need you. Get into our growing line, Hate.

[*Enter Jangle.*]

What's your name?

Jangle: It's Jangle: rhymes with dangle, tangle and wrangle.

Riot: Not to mention mangle. Stand by Hate, Jangle.

[*Enter Trouble.*]

Who are you?

Trouble: My name's Trouble. I'm the one for mischief. People have been trying to get rid of me for centuries—but they can't. I stick to the human race like glue.

Riot: My dear Trouble! We've been waiting for you. I've been wishing for you—and Pride's been sniffing for you, with that big nose of hers. Please join Jangle.

[*Enter Noise.*]

What do they call you?

Noise: Noise is the name. If you want it louder: NOISE! I'm the one for shattering people's nerves.

Riot: We shall certainly require your services. But try to keep quiet for the moment—and line up with our good friend Trouble.

[*Enter Discord.*]

What's your name, dearie?

Discord: Call me Discord. When I'm about nobody's in tune. I'm an expert at saying the right thing at the wrong time; and, of course, the wrong thing at the right time.

Riot: You strike the right note here. Please get into line. How many of us are here now? [*Counts.*] Eight, eh? You could call us the 'Orrible Octave!

Noise: When are we going to start the fun? I can't keep quiet much longer.

Riot: No. One, two, three—go!

[*Each character says his name in turn:* 'Riot! Greedy! Pride! Hate! Jangle! Trouble! Noise! Discord!' *They go up and down a crazy scale several times with their names, then shout them together as a mighty crescendo. Enter the Bellman. He carries eight bells on a stick. The eight characters roar with laughter at the sight of the Bellman. Suddenly, they become quiet.*]

Riot: And who on earth—are you?

Bellman: I am the Bellman.

Riot: The Bellman, eh? You'll be able to help us with all those bells. I'm sure Jangle and Noise will appreciate the din they will make.

Bellman: Yes, I want to help you. But not quite in the way you think. I am going to give each of you—a bell.

Riot: We don't mind. Do we, lads and lasses?

Chorus: Not a bit! Hurrah! Hurrah!

[*The Bellman gives each character an appropriate bell.*]

Bellman: Now, all of you—ring your bells.

[*They do so, shouting their names at the same time. There is a terrible din.*]

Jangle: [*when they have finished*] Oh—this is great. I loved that!

Noise: So did I.

Bellman: Now, I want us to try something else. Each of you, ring your bell—one after the other.

[*Daintily, they go up the scale—see Notes at end.*]
Now, go down again.

[*They do so. Then they go up and down several times, finishing off with a little shake of the bells.*]

Pride: Er—not bad!

Bellman: Now, we'll try a little tune. Look at this sheet of music: it will tell you what to do. Follow my stick!

[*They play a simple, well-known tune.*]

Discord: Well—I never thought we'd be able to do anything like that. It's the first time I've ever been in tune in my life!

Bellman: That's a good start. Now, I can teach you to play anything. What would you like?

Riot: It's Christmas time—not that I've much time for it, except for the turkey and crackers and the smashing noisy parties. Still, let's try something about Christmas.

[*They play another tune. When they have finished, they are very quiet.*]

Noise: [*quietly*] That was a Christmas carol, wasn't it? I liked that. Let's play another.

[*They do so.*]

Bellman: Shall we play some more?

Chorus: Yes! Yes!

[*They play one or two more carols.*]

Bellman: That was very good. Now, out there, many people have been listening—and taking notice of you. As we play our carols again, they are going to sing with us softly.

Riot: Stop! Stop! There's something we must do first!

Bellman: What's that, Riot?

Riot: We'll have to change our names. We can't sing Christmas carols with the descriptions we've got. Even I can see that's not right.

Bellman: I'm glad the suggestion has come from you, Riot—because, obviously, you're the leader. What would you like to call yourself?

Riot: Peace! Yes—I would like to be called Peace.

Bellman: What about you, Greedy?

Greedy: Helpfulness! I want to be Helpfulness.

Bellman: And you others: are you going to change, too?

Pride: My name was Pride—but I want it to be Modesty.

Hate: I was Hate. But now I want to be called Love.

Jangle: My name was Jangle; but I want it to be Serenity.

Trouble: People called me Trouble; but I want them to call me Happiness.

Noise: I was Noise. Now I want to be Quietness.

Discord: My name was Discord; but please call me—Harmony.

[*They turn their cards together.*]

Bellman: Now—you look much better. I think it would be a good idea if you said your *new* names once more. Let's go up and down the scale—and you say your names in turn—before we have the carols.

[*They do this:* ' Peace, Helpfulness, Modesty, Love, Serenity, Happiness, Quietness, Harmony; Harmony, Quietness, Happiness, Serenity, Love, Modesty, Helpfulness, Peace.']

Bellman: Now, we'll play our carols—and those people I've told you about will help us with their voices.

[*When the carols are finished, the characters come to front of stage. They repeat their new names, going up and down the scale. It is a good point to finish on the word ' Peace '.*]

Peace: [*turning to Bellman*] But, Mr Bellman—you've not changed your name yet?

Bellman: Thank you, Peace. I really hadn't thought of that. Let me think. . . . Yes, just call me the Christmas Bellman.

All: The Christmas Bellman!

Notes

1. A number of simple tunes and carols will have to be learned by the actors in order to fulfil the requirement of the play.

2. The notes of the bells should be in the same sequence as the names: Riot (C), Greedy (D), Pride (E), etc., up to Discord (top C).

3. If, instead of bells, recorders are used, the title of the play could be changed to 'The Christmas Piper'. There would, of course, have to be a few adjustments to the directions.

A CAUSE FOR CAROLS

by T. H. Ashcroft and D. H. Hedley

Cast

John	First Voice
Peter	Second Voice
Ruth	Third Voice
Linda	Fourth Voice
The Old Lady	Fifth Voice
The rest of the Carol Singers	Sixth Voice

[*The carol singers enter, led by a boy carrying a lighted lantern suspended from a long stick. They move to the first position—see Notes.*]

John: Let's see if we'll have any luck here.

Ruth: Can't be any worse than the last house. I'll never forget that man's big red face!

John: What shall we try here?

Peter: We'll make it 'While Shepherds Watched....' One, two, three!

[*They all sing, but are stopped after a few lines.*]

1st Voice: What's all this noise about? Don't you know that I'm watching my favourite programme—in colour? Anyway, here's 2p—but please go away!

[*John drops the coin in his bag. The carollers move on to the second position.*]

John: We're not doing very well tonight. Only 37p—so far.

Linda: This place looks hopeful. I like the curtains.

Peter: We'll try 'While Shepherds . . .' again. We made a bad start before. One, two, three!

[*Once more they are stopped after singing a few lines.*)

2nd Voice: Sorry, but I'm making a Christmas pudding—and I've just put all my spare small silver into it. You'll have to go. I must fly back to my pudding—and mince tarts!

[*They move to the third position. This time they are allowed to sing a little longer; but, presently, they are stopped with marked abruptness.*]

3rd Voice: Hey—I've got some friends inside, and we're listening to our new records. We *don't* want to listen to yours!

[*The young people move to the fourth position. They sing, but the reception is much the same as before.*]

4th Voice: This is a Bingo Club. We can't possibly listen to your stuff. We've all got our eyes down. But, here you are, here's a five-penny piece!

[*John drops the coin in his bag. They move to the fifth position. Reception as before.*]

5th Voice: Do we really have to have this sort of thing at Christmas? My family and I are sticking green stamps into our twenty-fifth book. My tongue's as dry as a board. We want all the presents we can get.

[*They move to sixth position. As before.*]

6th Voice: Buzz off!! [*A door slams.*]

[*The carollers move to the seventh position. This time, they sing their carol right through.*]

John: Would you believe it? Somebody's listening to us!

Ruth: Perhaps the house is empty?

Linda: No—I can see a little light.

Peter: Let's sing another carol then. One, two, three!

[*When they have sung their second carol, an Old Lady's voice is heard.*]

O. Lady: That carol was very beautiful. But, I am a very old lady—and I can't afford to give much. Could you please sing—just one more? I love to hear young people singing carols.

John: Of course we will.

[*They sing again.*]

O. Lady: Thank you—and God bless you.

All: A Merry Christmas! A Merry Christmas!

[*The carol singers, waving hands, move on a little way.*]

Peter: Stop! I don't like leaving the old lady like this. What can we do to help her?

John: She lives by herself—and you could see that she'd no money to spare.

Linda: I know. Let's give her *all* the money we've collected tonight!

Peter: That's a jolly good idea, Linda. We'll go back.
[They return to the Old Lady's home and sing one verse of a carol.]

O. Lady: How nice of you—singing to me again. Here is a little bit of something. I forgot to give it to you before.

Linda: Put it back into your purse. We're going to give something to *you*.

O. Lady: You already have. You have given me your Christmas Carols—and also your kindness.

John: We are going to give you all the money we've collected tonight. Here: please buy a little present for yourself.
[He holds out the bag.]

O. Lady: What a lovely thought, young man. You have made my Christmas a very happy one. But I *can't* take the money.

Ruth: We want you to take it!

O. Lady: No—no, thank you. There are many poor people who need it more than I do. I am not well off—but I can manage.

Linda: Are you *sure* you won't have it?

O. Lady: Quite sure. But the fact that you have thought of such a thing has meant more to me than all the money in the world.

John: What *can* we do with it, then? Any more bright ideas, Linda?

Linda: Yes. . . . Do you remember what the headmaster said at school about the children in the Children's Society Home? Let's send it to them!

O. Lady: A lovely thought.

John: Do you all agree?

All: Yes, yes!

Peter: But let's sing another carol for the old lady—before we go.
[They sing their last carol. Let this carol be appropriate—something about gifts.]

Notes

1. After singing in first position, the young people could move off stage, proceed round the back and reappear to take their places in the second position—and so on until they come to the seventh position. All the voices should be disembodied, except for hands which emerge from ' wings ' to offer coins.
2. Make up an optimum number of carol singers to go with John, Peter, Ruth and Linda. The boy with the lamp should be one of these extra singers.
3. Some boy, rough and gruff, should be chosen for the sixth voice.

Ann L. Stead offers opportunities for mime and dance in

THE FIRST CHRISTMAS TREE

Here, perhaps, is a more adventurous alternative to the Nativity play we so often see at Christmas. It is the legendary story of the Christmas tree. In order to create the maximum effect the children take the parts of the trees in the forest and thus all can be absorbed into the action.

There are two kinds of trees (although the children may be more than willing to make their own interpretations): first the dramatic ones with waving branches and swaying trunks, and then the stately pines with arms sloping gracefully outwards. As an accompaniment to the opening forest scene, either music or windy sound effects can be used. Elaborate costumes are not necessary for the trees; black jeans and sweaters are probably the best. In contrast to this, however, the pagans should be dressed as colourfully as possible, with a hoard of beads, bangles and rings worn over brightly coloured dresses.

Cast

Reader
Saint Boniface
Small boy for sacrifice
Pagan priest
Pagans 1, 2, 3, 4, 5
Tall oak tree
Small fir tree
Group of forest trees

Reader: If you were to look into most homes at this time of the year you could probably tell that it was Christmas, for somewhere there would be a sprig of holly, a bunch of mistletoe or a gaily decorated Christmas tree. The use of evergreens during this winter celebration goes right back to pagan times, when the druids used to worship with strange rituals and blood sacrifices. They had a feast at this time of the year and used evergreens for decoration, as a sign that there was life when all things seemed to be dead. The holly had special meaning for the early

Christians, who said that the red berries represented Christ's blood, and the prickly leaves were like his crown of thorns.

Many of you will know that Prince Albert, who was Queen Victoria's husband, brought the idea of a Christmas tree to England. He came from Germany, where people had decorated their homes with fir trees for many years. Just how they first came to think of the fir tree as a Christmas tree you are now about to see. We are going to take you deep into the heart of a German forest hundreds of years ago.

[*The curtains open on a dimly-lit stage. The trees are arranged in a not too orderly semi-circle, forming a forest clearing. In the centre of the semi-circle stands the tall oak tree; hidden behind it is the small fir tree. The trees are swaying about as the wind blows through them. Suddenly a drum begins to beat off-stage and the trees gradually stop their movements. The pagans, accompanied by the drum, walk slowly on to the stage in the following order: Priest, Pagan 1 with drum, Pagans 2 and 3 in a pair, the small boy with his hands tied behind his back, Pagans 4 and 5 in a pair. The boy is made to kneel before the oak tree, the others gather around. When everyone is in place the drummer stops. During the speaking the trees should move their arms to avoid cramp, but all movements must be slow and graceful.*]

Priest: This is the shortest day of the year when our Lord, the Sun, Ruler of the Skies, deserts us.

Pagan 1: We must show him our devotion.

Pagan 2: We must beseech him to return to his own.

Pagan 3: We shall offer him the gift of life. This boy will present our messages to the sun. He will prove our devotion.

Priest: Let us offer up our prayers to the Lord of the Skies.
[*All except the priest kneel down. They stretch out their arms.*]

Pagan 1: O Lord of the Skies, come back to us.

Pagan 2: Shine down and give us warmth and light.

All: O Lord of the Skies, come back to us.

Pagan 2: To you we offer the gift of life.

All: O Lord of the Skies, come back to us.
[*They all bow right down to the floor; the drum begins to beat slowly. They rise to their feet. The priest holds a dagger above the boy's head. The pagans begin to chant and the drumming speeds up until the priest has almost plunged the dagger into the boy.*]

All: Come back, come back, come back [*Enter Boniface. He starts as he realises what is about to happen*] come back. . . .

Boniface: Stop! [*The drumming and the chanting stop at once. He strides towards the priest.*] In the name of the true God, I command you to stop!

Pagan 4: Who are you, that you dare to interfere with our worship?

Boniface: My name is Boniface. I am a servant of the God of Love. He forbids all men to take life and he is the true Ruler of all the earth and the skies.

Pagan 5: Prove that what you say is true. If your God is so great, then he will help you to chop down this mighty tree with one blow from this axe.

[*Pagans laugh and jeer.*]

Boniface: I have faith in my God. Give me the axe. And take away this poor child.

[*He takes the axe from Pagan 5. Pagans 2 and 3 step forward and take the boy away from the tree. The other trees show great agitation as Boniface lifts the axe above his shoulder. He takes a slow, deliberate blow. The big tree sways faintly and then sinks to the ground. Thus is revealed the small fir tree. The rest of the trees stop their movement, with their arms curved towards the fir tree.*

All: Ah! [*They mutter and marvel among themselves.*]

Pagan 3: Look, another tree grows within its roots!

Pagan 5: It is a spruce fir!

Boniface: From this night forward that little tree shall be your holy emblem. It is the wood of peace, for you have built your homes of it. It is the sign of everlasting life, for its leaves are always green. It points to heaven and from this day it shall be called the tree of the Christ Child.

Priest: Release the boy. Go to your homes and dwell upon the words of this good man of God.

[*They release the boy and walk off slowly in different directions. Boniface watches them. When they have all gone he kneels down in thanksgiving, and as he does the curtains close upon him.*]

For Ruth Wood, the Nativity is not the end of the story but—as it should be—only the beginning. This play could well be used in church

JESUS IS KING

Hymn: ' O Little Town of Bethlehem ' verses 1, 2 and 5.
[*All sing. Joseph and Mary on stage with baby.*]

Narrator: Nearly two thousand years ago our Saviour came to earth,
And we are here today to show what happened at his birth.

Narrator 2: The inn was full, there was no room in Bethlehem that day.
So in a stable, in the gloom, Jesus the baby lay.
[*Some of the youngest children enter, stand behind the crib and sing* ' Away in a Manger.']

Narrator 1: Somehow the news that he was King travelled near and far,
And people came their gifts to bring, guided by a star.
[*Slowly, one by one, Shepherds enter, kneel and present their gifts, then the Kings, while the audience and children sing.*]

Hymn: ' O come, all ye faithful.'
[*Mary and Joseph leave stage carrying gifts; cast move to back of stage and sit quietly; disciples sit on ground and mend their nets.*]

Narrator 1: Jesus grew up and little's told about his childhood years,
But we know he shared with all men their laughter and their tears.
[*Jesus enters.*]

Narrator 2: And at last, when he was older, he began his ministry.
He soothed the sad, he healed the sick, he helped the blind to see.

Narrator 3: He called the rich, the poor, the proud, to help him with his teaching.
And fishermen and publicans were followers of his preaching.
[*Disciples move forward and sing* ' Fishers of Men '.]

Narrator 1: He loved the old, he loved the young, the wilful and the wild
But above all, he often said, he loved each trusting child.

Narrator 2: He talked of truth, he talked of faith, he showed men how to live,
How to behave and how to pray, to love and to forgive.

Hymn: ' Blest are the pure in heart.'

Narrator 1: Who was this man so humble, so reverenced and so praised?
Some folk began to question, and others were amazed.
[*Jesus slowly moves offstage. Crowds start moving into groups.*]

Narrator 3: The crowd became hysterical, started to shout and sing:
' Can this be our Messiah? Is this indeed our King? '

Hymn: ' All glory, laud and honour.' [*All the cast wave palms.*]

Narrator: But, oh, how quickly men can change—almost with their next breath,
The people mocked, the people scorned, shouting ' Put him to death '.
[*Crowd move to back of stage and sit.*]

Narrator: And darkness covered all the land when they set Barabbas free,
And sent instead our Lord to die, hanging on a tree.
[*Jesus walks slowly across stage carrying the cross and stands to one side.*]
[*Mary enters and kneels, weeping.*]

Hymn: ' There is a green hill.'
[*Jesus leaves stage towards end of hymn.*]

Narrator 3: We can feel with him the sorrow, the pain and misery,
But we know that he forgave us when he died for you and me.

Narrator 1: And the wonder of the story is the joy of Easter Day,
When he conquered death and showed us the truth, the life, the way.

Narrator 2: And later, when the time came for his earthly life to cease,
He sent his Holy Spirit to give comfort, strength and peace.

Hymn: ' Jesus, good above all other.'

[*Children take up positions for the Nativity scene again. Mary and Joseph sit with baby as before*.]

Adult Narrator: And now it's Christmas once again, the scene is as before.
It is a charming story, or is it something more?
And if Jesus dwells among us, do we treat him just the same?
Do we raise our hands in horror, do we hang our heads in shame?
Or shall we with the children, this Christmas, truly say
' O come to us, Lord Jesus, there is room for you today'?

Hymn: ' Thou didst leave thy throne.'

Prayers and Blessing.

Hymn: ' Once in royal David's city.'

'NO ROOM . . .'

A Christmas play by Anthony Davies, first acted by the children of his Solihull primary school. Size of cast is variable; the setting could be hall or church

Stage settings should be kept simple and unglamorised for all but the Herod's Palace scene, where some contrast would be an advantage. The play can be performed ' in the round '.

The Reader, whose part is important, should ideally stand at a lectern in view of the audience but off the stage. He or she can be spotlighted during readings.

In the original production the choir processed for ' Once in royal David's city ' from the rear of the hall to their places, with lighted candles. If this is done someone is required to collect candles, put them out and place them away safely.

Choir procession: ' Once in royal David's city.'

Reader: About 2,000 years ago a baby was born in Bethlehem. The place of his birth was a stable, crude, and no doubt unclean as stables often must be; but beautified as always by new birth and the promise of new life, and sanctified for ever because this was the Christ-child.

The story belongs to all time: past and present meet at the crib, and there, together, we shall find both a child and a challenge.

[*The above is read on a darkened stage, with Mary sitting in the shadows and a spotlight on the Reader. It is followed by a reading of Luke 1. 26–35, and 38. The spotlight goes off, the Reader departs. The angel Gabriel can appear on stage R, illuminated by slow spot. Lights up slowly for Mary to sing the Magnificat, verses 1–4, on a still dimly-lit stage. Stage darkens, Mary departs.*]

[*Glockenspiel plays children's theme music—see p. 73.*]

[*The children assemble on stage as if having a picnic. All settle down with their food.*]

1st child: Now, let's see. What have I got here? [*Examines his package and produces food.*]

2nd child: [*comes over.*] Very nice! Lovely! [*Looks in his own pack.*] How about this? [*Holds up a long loaf.*]

3rd child: Good gracious! What a long one!

[*The youngest child is busy feeding her Teddy bear. She suddenly gets hiccoughs violently.*]

1st child: Oh! you've done it again! You have been told before not to eat so quickly. Now you've got hiccoughs.

Youngest child: It's not me, it's him [*points to bear*].

2nd child: No dear, Teddy bears don't have hiccoughs. Now listen [*removes distracting bear*] take a deep breath and hold it until I say, ' Let go '.

[*Child holds breath; just as 2nd child is about to say ' Let go ', she blows out violently and sprays 2nd child with crumbs.*]

2nd child: Oh dear! That was naughty of you, Rachel [*wipes herself down*].

Youngest child: I'm sorry. . . . Well, it's cured my hiccoughs, anyway!

[*Another child runs in excitedly.*]

1st child: Hullo, what's up with you?

New child: I've heard a strange story.

Others: Have you?—Tell us, then—etc.

New child: I've heard a story that a baby is to be born in Bethlehem, over the hill there [*points*].

Youngest child: That's nice!

2nd child: But lots of children are born in Bethlehem.

New child: Yes, I know, but this one is going to be different.

Others: How? What do you mean? etc.

New child: It's all a bit of a muddle to me, but there is something about him being a king.

Youngest child: Oooh, that IS nice.

[*They fall silent for a moment.*]

1st child [*suddenly*]: Let's go and find him!

2nd child: But we couldn't—could we?

3rd child: We could . . . I think—we—could.

1st child: But what would they say at home?

2nd child: I don't know why, but somehow I don't think they would mind; not this time.

1st child: No, I don't think they would—not this time [*they gather up their things*].

3rd child: We must bring a present. [*They all agree.*]
[*As they depart, the youngest child hangs back.*]

Youngest child [*to bear*]: I don't know what my mum's going to say about this! Do you?

Others [*off stage*]: Come on!

Choir: 'The Broadway Carol.'
[*'Lonely child' theme music. The lonely or unwanted child slowly crosses a darkened stage, looks wistfully in the direction of the children's departure, and slowly and sadly returns and disappears.* *Music on p. 73.*]

Choir: 'People, look east.'

Reader: Luke 21–6. [*Cold wind sound effect, quietly. Cold light on stage. Enter Joseph, supporting Mary.*]

Joseph: Come on, Mary, my dear, you are so tired; we will rest here for a while.

Mary: I'm all right, Joseph, my dear, just a little tired. [*Joseph offers her something to drink.*]
We mustn't wait here very long. It's cold and lonely. [*Getting up.*] Come let's go; it can't be much further now.

Joseph: Very well. Let me help you. [*They go slowly together.*]
[*Quiet theme music for unwanted child, who crosses the back of stage alone, as if following Mary and Joseph hopefully.*]

Reader: Luke 2. 8–15.

Choir: 'Silent Night.'
[*The shepherds assemble on a darkened, coldly-lit stage. They warm themselves round fire.*]

1st Shep: It's cold tonight, very cold [*shivers*]. Even the fire doesn't seem to help very much.

2nd Shep: You are right there, Reuben. I'd rather be at home tonight.

3rd Shep: Me too! Think of it. Good food and a warm bed, instead of this.

4th Shep: Never mind, Benjamin. It is not always like this—praise be!

[*Another shepherd comes in flapping his arms. The others make room.*]

2nd Shep: Did you find your sheep? Is all well?

New Arrival: Yes, all's well, and the sheep are safe; but the lions are too near for comfort.

3rd Shep: Let's get some sleep while we can. [*They all settle down to sleep except the boy, who is restless. A light brightens very gradually, shining on shepherds only. The boy looks up fearfully, then in a panic, wakes the others. They all wake and hide their faces. The unseen angel speaks.*]

Angel: Do not be afraid. Listen. I bring you news of great joy, a joy to be shared by the whole people. Today in the town of David, a saviour has been born: he is Christ the Lord; and here is a sign for you; you will find a baby wrapped in swaddling clothes and lying in a manger.

Choir: The 'Gloria' (see page 73).

[*At the end of Gloria, light dims to previous strength.*]

1st Shep: Did you see that, or am I dreaming?—was there some-one there?

2nd Shep: There was someone, I'm sure . . . yes, I'm sure there was.

Boy: I was afraid to look, but I heard a voice.

Another Shep: So did I. What was it he said? 'Do not be afraid.' That's easy to say! I was scared—until he spoke—but only until he spoke.

3rd Shep: Yes, that's right, lad, as soon as he spoke I did not feel afraid at all.

4th Shep: 'Born this day in the town of David,' he said. That's Bethlehem—' a saviour, Christ' [*pause*] that's what he said . . . that's the great promise, don't you realise, it's the great promise! But I didn't really think it would happen this way.

Boy: 'YOU will find,' he said, too, 'YOU will find him. . . .' That means us . . . that means WE must go to Bethlehem, doesn't it? Now, to find him.

1st Shep: Yes, I suppose it does. Not easy, though.

2nd Shep: No, not easy, but I think you are right. What about the sheep?

Boy: Oh yes, the sheep . . . [*he pauses*].

2nd Shep: Come on, boy, but what? Speak up.

Boy: I was just thinking [*looks towards where the angel was*] that was a special kind of message, wasn't it? Well it was, wasn't it?

3rd Shep: Yes lad, that doesn't happen every day!

Boy [*continuing*]: Well in that case, if he [*waves towards angel*] sort of told us to go, then I think that somehow he will take care of the sheep. Does that sound silly?

3rd Shep: No, it doesn't. You know, I think the boy is right. Well done, lad! Come on, let's go.

[*As they go, the unwanted child can be seen in a darkened corner backstage, watching wistfully. As they finally depart, the child makes as if to follow, then turns back and goes off slowly. During this the 'lonely child' theme is heard.*]

Choir: ' O little town of Bethlehem.'

Reader: Luke 2. 7.

[*We are inside the inn. Servant maid is dusting. Knocking is heard off, maid pays no attention. Innkeeper's wife is heard off, ' See who is there, Martha!' Maid goes off and returns with Mary and Joseph.*]

Martha: I shall have to ask the master about this, sir, will you wait a minute? [*She goes off.*]

Innkeeper [*entering*]: What can I do for you? I'm very busy.

Joseph: We have come a long way. My wife is very weary. Can you find us a room or a place for my wife Mary to rest?

Innkeeper: I suppose you have come for the counting? Bethlehem is full of people who have come for the census. [*Wife comes in and listens, then speaks to Mary.*]

Wife: I don't think there is a room in Bethlehem anywhere.

Joseph: It doesn't sound very promising. Come on, Mary dear. We will have to go.

[*The wife has been talking to her husband.*]

Innkeeper: My wife suggests you could use the stable. It's not much. We can try to make it more comfortable; but there really is no room in the inn.

Joseph: Thank you. That's kind of you. Where is the stable, then?

[*They go out, the innkeeper leading the way. The maid is left dusting, shrugging her shoulders. The unwanted child creeps in* (*theme tune*), *but is sent off by the indignant maid.*]

[*Stage dimly lit. Set as if somewhere en route to Bethlehem. Children's theme music on glockenspiel. Group from first scene crosses stage slowly and uncertainly, the youngest child last, dragging bear.*]

1st child [*going back*]: Come on, dear, do hurry.

Youngest child: I'm tired.

1st child: I know but do come. Oh, just a little rest, then. It's not much further. [*They sit for a little while. One sings ' How far is it to Bethlehem?' They go off slowly. Glockenspiel music. Unwanted child half-crosses stage to follow and returns to theme music.*]

[*Stage set as interior of Herod's palace. A throne is enough to give the effect. Fairly high lighting.*]

Reader: Matthew 2. 1–8.

Choir: ' Unto us is born a Son.'

[Two young palace retainers are playing about in the absence of authority.]

1st boy: I wonder what's on today, and how long we'll be standing here.

2nd boy: Let's hope he's in a good mood. You never know, do you?

1st boy: How very true! There is a rumour going round that we are having special visitors; something unusual, but you know what rumours are around here!

2nd boy: Look out! Here comes the chief! *[They stand to attention each side of the chair. Enter the captain of the guard.]*

Captain: Seeing that you have so much time to gossip, perhaps you can spare a moment to do your job properly. Unless of course you would like me to. . . ?

Boys *[bowing frantically]*: No sir, no, no, etc.

Captain: That's better!

[Music for the entry of Herod. Retainers, chief minister. Entry, if possible, from somewhere in auditorium. Stage brightens.]

Herod: Well, chief minister, have you got to the bottom of this business? A star in the east; King of the Jews; the whole of Jerusalem is full of rumours, of prophesies, and tales of this Christ. What have you done about it?

C. Min: May it please your Majesty, the so-called wise men, the royal travellers, are outside, awaiting audience with your Majesty as arranged.

Herod: Right. Bring them in then *[more bowing]*. Get on with it. Perhaps we can put an end to this business before it gets out of hand.

[Percussion for entry of wise men. They are announced in turn with ceremony; Melchior, Caspar, Balthazar. They bow in unison.]

Wise Men *[together]*: Greeting!

Herod: We welcome you to Jerusalem, and wish to hear your stories—and where your journey leads you.

Wise Men *[sharing the words]*: We follow a star, O Herod . . . Which will lead us to the child . . . The holy and royal child for whom we seek.

Herod [*looking thoughtful*]: Go then; go to Bethlehem and there seek this child, this king you speak of. Seek for him carefully—
[*He dismisses them with a wave; as they bow to go, he adds*]—and when you find him, bring news back to me. Come and tell me where you find him, *exactly* where you find him, so that I can go and see also . . . and worship this child.
[*The wise men depart. Percussion music.*]

Herod: And listen, all of you. Not one word of this to anyone. Do you understand? Not one word outside—and you know what happens if I am displeased! [*Herod departs, to his music. The remainder depart, boys last.*]

Choir: ' In the bleak midwinter ' (not last verse).

Reader: Matthew 2. 9.
[*Mary and Joseph are in the stable; Mary is seated in front of deep crib with Joseph standing behind. Stage dimly lit; soft warm light faintly on Mary. Voices are heard from rear of hall and the Shepherds approach, walking slowly and pausing occasionally.*]

1st Shep: I think we have found the place.

2nd Shep: Yes, there is a light ahead. Come on, lad, we have found the baby.

Boy: Oh good! You mean the baby who is Christ the Lord, not an ordinary baby.

3rd Shep: No, not an ordinary baby.

Boy: That will be the mother sitting by the crib; she looks very peaceful—she's very beautiful, isn't she?

1st Shep: Yes, she is very beautiful. How proud they look. I'm glad we came.

4th Shep [*as they walk*]: Let's make our presents to the baby.
[*The shepherds approach the crib in turn, kneeling very slowly.*]

1st Shep [*giving a flask*]: Perhaps one day he will be thirsty.

2nd Shep [*giving fleece*]: Perhaps one day he will be cold.

3rd Shep and Boy [*giving pillow*]: Perhaps one day he will need somewhere to lay his head.
[*Mary reacts with some anxiety while shepherds take their places in tableau. The unwanted child creeps in (theme music) but is shooed off by innkeeper's wife who comes in with armful of straw.*]

Choir: ' The Infant King ' or ' What child is this? '

[*Lively music is heard for arrival of wise men, in contrast to simplicity of shepherds' arrival. The Wise Men's procession arrives, down centre of hall, and they present their gifts. This can be done either in slow and dignified mime, or each can be announced with fanfare, etc.*]

Choir: ' The Zither Carol.'

[*The children's glockenspiel theme music. The children's voices are heard from rear of hall.*]

1st child: How much further? I didn't think it was as far as this.

2nd child: I've lost my present. It's gone. I must have dropped it.

3rd child: Here it is. Hold on to it.

2nd child: Where is Rachel? Come on, dear. Let me help you. Shall I carry Teddy for you?

Youngest child: No thank you, I can manage, but I wish Teddy bears could walk by themselves. It does get a bit hard sometimes—oooh! Look!

1st child: We've found him; we've found the baby!

2nd child: We've done it; but—just—look!

3rd child: Look at those gentlemen all dressed up! Look at their clothes!

1st child: And those other men—shepherds, I think they are.

Youngest child: But where's the baby? That's who we really came for.

1st child [*in loud whisper*]: Come on; let's go nearer.

[*They approach slowly, with wonder, go to the front of the stage, kneel or sit round the crib, and shyly place their presents. The youngest child comes last; she gazes up at one of the wise men and shows him her Teddy bear; she then sits near the crib.*]

Solo group [*sings*]: ' What can I give him? ' (last verse of ' In the bleak midwinter ').

[*When all are settled, the unwanted child creeps to the front of the stage and sits there doubtfully. ' Lonely child ' music, quietly. This time no-one seems to mind. Mary sees the unwanted child, and motions the youngest child to go and bring him to the crib. The youngest child takes him by the hand and leads him to a place near Mary. The unwanted child looks up at Mary and, for the first time, smiles.*]

Choir: ' Sleep my Saviour ' or other lullaby.

[*Full lighting*.]

All stand and sing ' O come, all ye faithful.'

[*The audience then sits and the cast retires, led by Mary cradling her (mimed) baby, Joseph and the unwanted child walking between them looking happy. Finally the choir retires, to the piano accompaniment of a miscellany of music used in the play*.]

CHRISTMAS EVE, 1818

Joan Kendall's sketch could be used as an interlude in a carol service or as the basis of a project on the stories behind well-known Christmas carols

[*Frau Schmidt is waiting for her two children to come back from choir practice. She has supper ready for them. They arrive in big scarves and woolly hats and gloves.*]

Frau S.: Oh, there you are, children. Shut the door and come in quick. You must be very cold after your walk through the snow.

[*Children take off their outdoor things.*]

Johann: It's beautiful outside, Mum. It's stopped snowing now, and the moonlight makes the snow sparkle like anything.

Maria: I'm longing to go back again for the midnight service. How long is it before we start?

Frau S.: It won't be long now. Drink up your hot lemon and eat your bread and honey. You had a very long choir practice tonight—I expected you earlier.

Johann: The organ's broken, Mum.

Frau S.: The *organ's* broken? That's terrible. What went wrong?

Maria: It was a MOUSE! [*She giggles.*]

Johann: Yes, a mouse nibbled through the leather of the bellows and they won't blow!

Frau S.: It's all very well your laughing, but this is very serious. Pastor Mohr is a very musical man, and he will be quite upset if there is no music for the midnight service, and so will Herr Gruber.

Johann: It's all right Mum, there *will* be music.

Maria: Yes, lovely, *different* music. That's why we were late home.

Frau S.: I think I had better sit down and let you explain.

Children: WELL. . . .

Maria: All right, Johann, you tell her.

Johann: The other night Pastor Mohr was walking home through the snow thinking how quiet and still our village looked. He thought it might have been just like this in Bethlehem the night Jesus was born.

Maria: And he made up a poem about it and as soon as he got home he wrote it down on a piece of paper. He was so excited that he went out again in the snow and walked all the way to Herr Gruber's house in Arnsdorf.

Johann: And Herr Gruber liked it so much that he made up a tune for it and played it on his guitar.

Maria: And they taught it to us at choir practice and *that's* what we're going to have tonight!

Frau S.: Well, I *am* surprised! Fancy all that happening just because a mouse nibbled the leather! It will be quite exciting to hear this new carol—and I certainly didn't know Herr Gruber could play the guitar! Finish up your supper now, and we'll get going.

[*They all put on outdoor things and set off through the organ vestry, down the North aisle and up the centre. The children sit with the rest of the choir in the choir stalls, and Frau S. with the congregation.*]

Pastor Mohr [*coming forward and addressing the congregation*]: My dear people, we have come together in our lovely church in our beloved land of Austria to celebrate the birth of our Lord Jesus Christ. As some of you will have heard, our organ is not available—surely for the first time for very many years. But we have music for you of a different kind. My friend Herr Gruber will play for you and we will do our best to sing you a new Carol:

[*To guitar accompaniment, the choir sing*]

Choir: ' Silent night, holy night. . . .'

THE WOOD SPEAKS

A play for Advent by Nigel Sustins for the 10–14 age range which relates the Christmas and Easter stories

Characters:

The Old Carpenter.
The Innkeeper.
The Innkeeper's Wife.
Four Shepherds.
King Herod.
Two Soldiers.
Foreign Prince.
Prince's Servant.
Joseph.
Mary.
Two Roman Soldiers.
Voice (off-stage).

SCENE 1: BETHLEHEM, OUTSIDE THE INN

Innkeeper's Wife: Come along, Husband. In a few months we shall have many visitors coming to stay in Bethlehem. We must make our Inn look clean and tidy. Think of all the painting jobs there are to do, and repairs to begin.

Innkeeper: Don't fuss, Wife. We needn't worry yet. Nobody else gets as excited as you do this early.

Wife: I don't want you to leave everything to the last minute, that's all.

[*Old Carpenter enters and walks up to Innkeeper and Wife.*]

Carpenter: Good morning, Friends. Did I hear somebody say there were repairs to be done?

Innkeeper: You must have long ears if you did. Suppose there are; *you* don't look strong enough to lift a hammer.

Carpenter: I'm a skilled carpenter. I've been a carpenter all my working life, and can work wonders with a few simple pieces of wood. Just try me out.

Wife: We can't trust him with any important jobs, Husband. But there's the old feed-trough in the stable that wants patching up. He can mend that to earn himself a bowl of soup.

Carpenter: I'll do anything you like. Just show me the way.

Innkeeper: The stable's over there [*points*]. Let's see what sort of job you make of the trough, then.

[*Carpenter walks across to right of stage, where there is a broken trough. He gets his tools out and starts work.*]

Carpenter: [*as he works*] Every piece of wood is different. If only wood could speak, think of all the tales it might tell.

Voice: [*from offstage*] Listen!

Carpenter: [*alarmed*] What was that? Who spoke?

Voice: It is the voice of the wood that speaks. From now on, you will be able to hear what the wood says.

Carpenter: [*looking at the trough*] How can the wood be speaking? I don't understand.

Voice: All your life you have worked faithfully, not minding the humble and the dirty jobs. Now you shall be rewarded. I am coming to this earth. I too shall be a carpenter like you. But first of all, I shall be a baby, and this trough you are mending shall be my cradle.

Carpenter: But who are you? I don't know you.

Voice: I am the One who lives for ever, and who saves the sons of men.

[*Carpenter covers his eyes, and bows to ground. Then he looks up at the trough.*]

Carpenter: It looks as though the wood were on fire. But it's unharmed. [*He touches it and burns his fingers.*] Ow! it's red hot!

[*Carpenter gets up, and rushes across to Innkeeper and Wife.*]

Carpenter: I've just heard a voice! It came out of the wood!

Innkeeper: What are you babbling about?

Carpenter: There's a baby going to be cradled in the trough I've mended! The Voice said so!

Wife: He's mad. Pay him, and then he can get on his way.

Carpenter: How wonderful that it should be *me*! . . . [*Exit.*]

Innkeeper: He didn't even wait for his money, crazy old man!

[*Innkeeper and Wife exit.*]

SCENE 2: FIELDS OUTSIDE BETHLEHEM

[*Night. Four Shepherds sit looking after their sheep in front of a fire.*]

1st Shepherd: How cold the nights get. I put on thicker coats and pile the fire higher, but still I freeze.

2nd Shepherd: Don't complain too much. You could be worse off. You're not in prison, are you, or wandering around the countryside homeless?

3rd Shepherd: Talking about wandering people, there's someone coming this way. He looks as if he might be a tramp.

4th Shepherd: He must be mad to be out in this weather, whoever he is.

[*Enter Carpenter.*]

1st Shepherd: Good evening, Grandfather. Have you come to choose yourself a nice woolly sheep for a pillow tonight?

Carpenter: [*sitting down with them*]. I'm travelling towards the next village. I prefer to travel at night, when the roads are empty. You don't mind if I share your fire a moment?

2nd Shepherd: Go ahead. What do you do for a living?

Carpenter: I'm a carpenter; have been for forty years.

3rd Shepherd: You look as if you might have a story to tell us, to shorten the night a little.

Carpenter: I could tell you a story to make you sit up.

4th Shepherd: Come on, then, let's hear it.

Carpenter: Today I was in Bethlehem. I was mending a feed-trough in a stable when I heard a voice.

1st Shepherd: Oh, we hear voices too. They're usually just in the wind, not real.

Carpenter: This was real. Somebody special is going to be born, it told me, down in the village. Somebody who will grow up to surprise everyone.

2nd Shepherd: Don't believe such stories, old man. Nothing special ever happens. We sit here night after night, and the same wind blows; the same sheep bleat in our ears. We're sick of it.

Carpenter: Give me your crook a moment.

2nd Shepherd: My crook! Why?

Carpenter: It's made of wood. I can tell what the wood says!
[*Shepherd hands over his crook. Carpenter feels it carefully.*]

3rd Shepherd: What does it tell you?

Carpenter: This wood speaks about great joy, about a dark night suddenly made brilliant. You will see the baby I told you of. It might be many months away, but you will kneel beside the cradle I mended for him.

4th Shepherd: How can a piece of wood tell you that? [*laughs*].

Carpenter: You will not laugh when it happens. Now I must go.
[*Gets up.*]

1st Shepherd: [*when Carpenter has gone*]. Some people believe anything. Let's forget mad old men, and put some more wood on the fire.

SCENE 3: KING HEROD'S PALACE

[*Herod sits on his throne, holding a long wooden staff. Two Soldiers enter, bringing in Carpenter.*]

1st Soldier: Great King, we have brought the old carpenter you wish to question.

Herod: Thank you, guards. Where did you find him?

2nd Soldier: In the Market Place, telling his stories as usual, my Lord Herod.

Herod: Step forward, old man.
[*Carpenter comes forward and kneels.*]

Herod: These stories you tell, how can you really believe them?

Carpenter: I do not lie, my King. The stories are true.

Herod: [*sneers*]. About a baby who is soon to be born, who will save men and women? What will he save them from?

Carpenter: From all that is wrong.

Herod: [*standing up, and leaning on his staff*]. I am the King! I and the Romans rule this land. Are you saying that we rule in the wrong way?

Carpenter: There is much that is wrong which the King cannot stop.

Herod: I do not believe these stories. They are harmful. Unless you stop telling them, you will be put in prison.

Carpenter: [*pleads*]. No, my Lord! I am too old for prison! [*Grasps Herod's wooden staff.*] Ah! You will not! You cannot!

Herod: What do you mean?

Carpenter: The wood of your staff, it speaks. It tells me you will try to kill the little baby; you—the King!

Herod: When will you stop talking nonsense? Guards! Take him out! [*to Carpenter*]. You can go for now, but don't tell your stories again. One of you men stay behind.

[*1st Soldier takes Carpenter out. 2nd Soldier stays with Herod.*]

Herod: Follow the old fool. He is a dangerous liar. You know what to do when no one else can see what is happening.

2nd Soldier: Yes, Lord. We will do it quietly. [*Exit.*]

SCENE 4: A LONELY PLACE

[*Enter Carpenter. He looks around him. Suddenly, Two Soldiers rush on with swords drawn. Prince and his Servant step out from other side of stage and face Soldiers. After a slight clash of swords, Soldiers run offstage.*]

Prince: [*sheathing sword*]. See the cowards run! Why should they want to attack you, old man?

Carpenter: Because I told stories that displeased the King.

Prince: Well, I am like a king in my own land, and I do not mind stories.

Carpenter: Who are you then, Sir?

Prince: I am a traveller from distant parts, newly arrived here with my servants. I think I have come too early, for the signs in the sky that I watch for are not yet right. In my own land, I saw the stars and planets in their great dance, and they told me a King was soon to be born in Israel. So I have come. But it seems that he is not yet born.

Carpenter: I too know of this King. I do not think you will have long to wait now.

Prince: I have a gift for him [*to the Servant*]. Mahal, bring the wooden chest.

[*Servant brings the chest across to Carpenter, who touches it.*]

Carpenter: Yes, this wood speaks to me. The young King *will* receive your gift.

Prince: May it be soon. The world is waiting for him. [*Exit.*]

SCENE 5: BESIDE A ROAD

[*Carpenter is asleep beside a road. Joseph and Mary enter, and stop for a rest.*]

Joseph: Let us rest here, my love. The donkey can graze for a little while.

Mary: It is so hot on the road today. How far to the village?

Joseph: Bethlehem is about five miles away. We shall be there before evening.

Mary: This good old man sleeps sound. I hope he has sweet dreams.

Carpenter: [*waking up*]. Oh, I have company! It was so hot that I had to rest for a few minutes. Are you on your way to Bethlehem too?

Joseph: Yes; my wife, Mary and I are due there tonight.

Carpenter: It will be very crowded, but I expect you know that.

Mary: Yes, I can't help wondering where we'll sleep.

Joseph: We'll find somewhere. Do you live in Bethlehem?

Carpenter: No. but I often go there looking for work. I'm a carpenter.

Joseph: Are you? I ought to have seen it, eh? I am too, Joseph, of Nazareth.

Carpenter: Oh yes, I've heard of you. I heard news of your wedding too.

Joseph: We're both looking forward to our first child.

Carpenter: What will you call your little child, good woman?

Mary: Oh, I have a name for him. It will suit him. Look, I have a toy ready for him. Joseph made it. [*She hands the Carpenter a wooden toy.*]

Carpenter: But . . . but . . . it can't be! Your baby! It is to be *your* baby!

Joseph: Why are you so surprised?

Carpenter: This toy. . . . *He* will hold it!

Joseph: Well, we must really be getting on now. Thanks for the talk, Carpenter.

Carpenter: [*giving the toy back to Mary*]. Don't forget this. *He'll* need it. Goodbye. God bless you. [*Exit.*]

Mary: He was a strange man. Rather nice though. What did he mean? It was almost as if he knew.

Joseph: Oh, I think perhaps he did. Let's hope many more people will come to know. Well, let's find the donkey and be on our way to Bethlehem. [*Exit.*]

SCENE 6: IN A WOODED PLACE NEAR JERUSALEM

[*The Wooded Place can be suggested by a painted backdrop of trees, or cardboard shapes. One tree, centre stage, must be detached from the background. The Carpenter, now very old, rests between the trees. Enter Two Roman Soldiers.*]

1st Soldier: These trees look just right.

2nd Soldier: They certainly do. Good, stout branches and trunks.

1st Soldier: There's an old man over there. Here—move away from these trees; they'll soon be coming down!

Carpenter: Coming down? What do you need them for?

2nd Soldier: They'll be made into crosses to hang criminals on, up in Jerusalem.

Carpenter: The wood won't take kindly to that. Here it's been, year after year, doing no one harm, and now you're going to turn it to a bad use.

1st Soldiers: Criminals have to die somehow. The cross happens to be the Roman way.

Carpenter: All the same, it can't give a carpenter much joy to make those things. I've been a carpenter for many years, and I've always put the wood to a good use.

2nd Soldier: We can't stand here being wet-eyed over a tree! Out of the way!

[*The Soldiers set to work cutting at the central tree.*]

Carpenter: [*touching the tree they are cutting*]. Stop! The tree . . . it is speaking!

1st Soldier: What are you saying? So the tree's got a voice, has it?

Carpenter: I have the gift of hearing what it says. Once—a long time ago now—I mended a wooden trough to hold a special child. He must be full grown, and a man at last. But this wood speaks of his . . . death!

2nd Soldier: You're mad! Stand clear!

Carpenter: [*feeling 1st Soldier's wrist*]. The wood tells me something about you too. One day, quite soon, you will be promoted to Centurion, and you will see the Young King die. You will recognise him. He will die on this tree!

1st Soldier: But this tree will be made into crosses.

Carpenter: Then he must be going to die—on a cross!

2nd Soldier: Whatever is all this rubbish about? Let's go on somewhere else, and come back when the old fool has gone. [*Soldiers go out.*]

Carpenter: I don't understand. He was going to have a happy, important life. He can't die as a criminal. . . .

Voice: Listen! It is the Voice of the Wood that speaks. Don't be mistaken. This is all part of the plan. I was born into a wooden cradle, and I shall die on a wooden cross. But there will be victory and freedom for all men when I have died. Where the tree is split and felled, there a sapling sprouts up full of new life. I will be Lord for all time, but first I must die on a cross of wood.

Carpenter: You have spoken to me again! And the tree—it glowed like Moses' burning bush! Now I see more clearly, and I shall not die in misery. My life has come to a happy close.

[*He sleeps beneath the centre tree.*]

CURTAIN

A play devised for the children of Bridget Crowe's group in Plymstock, which firmly links the Nativity story with both past and present

'JESUS IS ALIVE!'

Introduction

'O come, all ye faithful', *verses 1, 2, 3, sung by whole congregation.*

SCENE 1

Rachel: It is very nearly Christmas—what are we going to do this year?

Michael: What do you mean, *do*? Why should we do anything?

Margaret: Well, we always do something, don't we? We go carol singing or make up parcels for the old people or decorate the hall or something, just to remember that it *is* Christmas.

Rachel: Let's do a nativity play. We haven't done one for ages.

Margaret: What a good idea! It shouldn't be very difficult, because the story has already been written and we all know it.

Michael: I wish we could have a new story. I get a bit bored with the same old thing.

Margaret: Don't be silly. You can't have a nativity play with a different story. Nativity means birth, and we all know who is supposed to be born.

Michael: OK then, let's do one, but bags I not to be dressed up like an angel or something.

Rachel: That's all right, there's lots of others who like getting dressed up—so here goes.
[*Readers enter—walk to place to tune of* 'Living Lord'.]

The Mime of the Nativity

[*Children mime the nativity scenes as the readers tell the story.*]

Reader A: God loves all the people on earth. He loves them so much that he sent his son from heaven to earth. God's son came to be our brother and to tell us that God is our father too. The only Son of God is our Lord Jesus Christ.

Reader B: It happened long ago: nearly two thousand years ago. People lived on earth for a long time before our Lord Jesus was born. They tried to know God, but they had strange ideas about him. They were afraid of God. They did not know that God is our Father who loves us. But God had a plan to help men to know him. For this purpose he chose one race of people—the Jews. He called the Jews ' God's chosen people '.

[*Mime begins.*]

Reader C: At last the time came when God began to act upon his plan to send the Saviour to earth: his own Son, our Lord Jesus. God had chosen a mother for Jesus; Mary, the holiest of women. Like all good Jewish girls she knew a good deal about God's plan. Mary was waiting for the Saviour's coming and praying earnestly for it.

Reader D: Mary lived in Nazareth in the province of Galilee. God sent an angel to her, the archangel Gabriel. Gabriel went in to Mary and said: ' Hail, Mary, full of grace, the Lord is with thee.' Mary was puzzled. She asked herself what the angel could mean. The angel said: ' Do not be afraid, Mary, you are to have a child from God. You are to call him Jesus. He is the Son of God. He will be a king forever. '

When the angel had finished explaining, Mary said: ' I am ready to do all that God asks of me.' Then the angel returned to God.

Reader A: Mary was going to marry Joseph. Joseph also knew that the Saviour was coming, but he did not know yet that it was about to happen, and that Mary was going to be the Saviour's mother.

Reader B: The Roman emperor called for a census of all his empire. All the Jews had to give in their names at the cities from which their families came. Joseph and Mary were of the family of King David. David's city was Bethlehem.

Reader: So they had to go on a journey from Nazareth to Bethlehem. This meant they had to go right across the country. It was a long journey. It took a good three days.
At last they reached Bethlehem. It was evening. They looked for a place in which to spend the night but there was no room in the inn.

Reader D: Mary and Joseph went into a cave; this cave was sometimes used as a stable and it had a manger from which the animals ate. In this stable Jesus Christ was born.

Hymn: 'O little town of Bethlehem' [*first three verses, in which congregation join.*]

Reader A: Round about Bethlehem there were a lot of sheep. At night they stayed out in the open with the shepherds who looked after them. Suddenly an angel stood before the shepherds, radiant with light. The shepherds shrank away from him in fear. The angel said:

Reader B: 'Fear not: I bring you good news of great joy for all the people. Tonight your Saviour is born in the city of David. Go and see for yourselves. You will find the child wrapped in swaddling bands and lying in a manger.'

Reader C: All at once the sky was filled with angels. They sang: 'Glory to God in the Highest and peace to his people on earth.' Then they went back to heaven and the shepherds saw them no more. Then the shepherds said to each other: 'Come, let us go over to Bethlehem, as God's messenger has told us, and see what has happened.'
Quickly the shepherds hurried along the way. And . . . yes! They found Mary and Joseph, and the child in the manger. They were happy.

Reader D: There is a story that while Jesus was in Bethlehem, some important visitors came to see him: three wise men from the East. These three wise men were astrologers. This means that they could tell by the stars what was going to happen on earth. They had seen by the stars that a king was to be born in the Jewish land. They were not Jews. But God sent his son to earth to tell *all* men that they are God's children.

Reader A: The three wise men set off for Bethlehem. They were filled with joy when they saw the star moving on until it came to the place where Mary and Joseph were living with Jesus. There the star stood still.

Reader B: The three wise men entered. They saw Jesus. They recognised him as the great king for whose sake they had made their long journey. They worshipped Jesus.

[*All cast sing verse 1* of '*Living Lord*'.
Enter infants, around tableau of the Nativity. They sing 'Away in a manger'. Exit infants.]

SCENE 2

Rachel: That's all very well, but that all happened ages ago. What's that go to do with us?

Margaret: Well, it's a nice story, isn't it? I love stories about babies and pretty angels, and didn't Joseph take care of Mary nicely?

Rachel: Yes. I liked it. Didn't the little children look sweet singing to Jesus?

Michael: That wasn't Jesus, that was just a big doll.

Margaret: Yes, but it really did happen, didn't it? It is not just a fairy story.

Rachel: Of course not. Didn't you hear the children sing 'I ask thee to stay close by me for ever, and love me I pray'? That means that Jesus is still alive now and will look after us.

Michael: I don't know what that means. If he was born 2,000 years ago he can't be still alive now.

Margaret: That's where you are wrong. We've been learning all about just where we can find Jesus and you would be surprised just how often you can meet him.

Michael: Don't be silly. You can't meet him anywhere around Plymstock [*insert name of home town*], he died in Jerusalem thousands of years ago.

Rachel: Well I think you can. Whenever you go to church on Sunday morning, you meet Jesus in the bread and wine.

Michael: How can Jesus be there?

Margaret: We don't really understand but we know it is true, because he told us about it the night before he died. On that night he met his special friends and they sat down to a meal.

The Mime of the Eucharist

[*Children mime Last Supper and Eucharist as the Readers tell the story.*]

[*Enter Jesus and his friends to tune of 'Living Lord'. They stand round the table.*]

Reader A: For in the same night that he was betrayed, he took bread and after giving thanks, he broke it, gave it to his disciples, and said. 'Take, eat; this is my body which is given for you. Do this in remembrance of me.' Again, after supper he took the cup; he gave thanks, and gave it to them, saying ' Drink this, all of you; for this is my blood of the new Covenant, which is shed for you and for many, for the forgiveness of sins. Do this, as often as you drink it, in remembrance of me '.

Reader C: Because Jesus told us to, Christians have done this ever since.

[*Exit Jesus and his friends.*]

[*Enter priest and congregation, who stand around table.*]

Reader D: For in the same night that he was betrayed, he took bread; and after giving thanks, he broke it, gave it to his disciples, and said, ' Take, eat, this is my body which is given for you. Do this in remembrance of me '. Again, after supper he took the cup; he gave thanks, and gave it to them, saying, ' Drink this, all of you; for this is my blood of the new Covenant, which is shed for you and for many, for the forgiveness of sins. Do this, as often as you drink it, in remembrance of me.'

[*All cast sing: ' Blessing and honour and glory and power be yours for ever and ever. Amen.'*]

[*All cast sing Verse* 2 *of ' Living Lord '.*]

[*All go out.*]

SCENE 3

Margaret: Now do you see, Michael? On Christmas Day we can come to church to love Jesus who is alive beneath the forms of bread and wine, just as 2,000 years ago he was alive beneath the form of a tiny baby.

Michael: All right, I grant you that. Jesus is alive and we can meet him in the Eucharist. But is that all?

Rachel: Of course it's not. There was something else we learnt about in Sunday school. Do you remember that bit about ' when we help other people, it is the same as helping Jesus '?

Margaret: Yes. It says that if someone is really hungry and we give him something to eat, it is the same as giving food to Jesus.

Michael: That's a bit strange, isn't it? Do you honestly mean that if I met a dirty old tramp and gave him a drink of water it would be the same as giving water to Jesus?

Margaret: Yes. And what's more, if you *didn't* give him any water, that would be just like saying no to Jesus.

Rachel: But what sort of people are these who need help from other people?

Mime of those in need

[*Children mime help given to those in need.*]

Reader A: I was hungry and you gave me food;

Reader B: I was thirsty and you gave me drink;

Reader C: I was a foreigner and you took me home with you;

Reader D: I was in rags and you gave me clothes;

Reader A: I fell ill and you looked after me;

Reader B: I was in prison and you came to see me.

Reader C: Believe me—when you helped the least of my brothers, you helped me.

Hymn: [*All sing*] 'When I needed a neighbour. . . .'

[*Enter infants—They sing 'Little Jesus sweetly sleep'.*]

[*All go out.*]

SCENE 4

Michael: That makes me feel awful. If I say I love Jesus I should want to help him. But I never see anyone who is really hungry or thirsty, so how can I help them?

Rachel: There's a lot of ways. Visiting a lonely person is like visiting Jesus, and you must know some of those; there's plenty of them.

Margaret: Haven't you heard about all the thousands of people who haven't got a proper house to live in? You could help *them*.

Michael: How? I haven't got a house to give away.

Rachel: But you could save up some of your pocket money and bring it to church on Christmas Day.

Margaret: Yes—they're going to have a collection after every service on Christmas Day and send the money to Shelter, which helps homeless people.

Michael: So *we* can be just like the shepherds and wise men, 2,000 years ago—we can bring our love and presents on Christmas Day and give them both to our Living Lord.

[*Enter whole cast to set up tableaux, with posters advertising Shelter collection as background.*]

Hymn: [*All sing ' Living Lord ', verses* 1, 3, *and* 4.]

Prayer: Living Lord God,

We are glad that we know the real meaning of Christmas. Thank you for coming into the world on Christmas Day. We pray for all the people who do not know you; For all who ignore you, keeping Christmas for themselves. We have nothing to give you except our love, but we want to give as much of this as we can. We know that when we love other people, we are also loving you. Please help us to do this. In the name of Jesus. Amen.

'STANDING IN THE RAIN . . .'

The carol service at John Peers' church in County Durham made a break with the usual tradition

Each year we try to present the Christmas message with a different slant in the context of a Christmas Eve carol service, and to make full use of our church-attending children in the process.

On one occasion we decided to pinpoint contemporary situations into which the child Jesus might well have been born. First of all we set the traditional scene in word and mime, between carols, before moving forward into a present-day situation.

A reading which illustrated the setting of a typical Palestinian courtyard near an inn was immediately followed by the Birth narrative from St Luke's Gospel. A few of our kindergarten children then mimed the story to each verse of ' Mary's Boy-Child ', sung by a folk group formed from our Sunday night youth club. All the action took place on a portable stage in front of the chancel screen, which was curtained to form a back-cloth, and on the curtains we displayed ' appeal ' posters issued by such charities as Oxfam and Christian Aid.

From the traditional we moved to the present by way of a rather, florid sermon preached by myself, which painted the Nativity Story in sentimental colours. Meanwhile, between the paragraphs, an interrupting adult shouted out very relevant contrasting data in order to draw people's attention to the real situation; and factual information about similar contemporary situations was thrown in. During all this the preacher continued as if the interruptions were not taking place. Special reference to Britain's paltry aid to developing countries was made by the interrupter, and this was compared with statistics relating to our own self-indulgence in the past year. At the end of this episode the interrupter leaped onto the stage to recite Sydney Carter's poem, ' The Present Tense ', and both he and I sang ' Sing we the Song of High Revolt ', from *New Life*, to the tune of ' Tannenbaum '.

Following the next carol, members of the GFS mimed the carol ' Standing in the Rain '. A few sat at a table to represent Britain and the West, and during each verse two other members came on stage trying to attract their attention to their own particular plight, but in vain. The theme of each scene was slotted into a hymn board as it was depicted: i.e. ' No home ', ' No country ', ' No food ', etc. Each verse was read out loud for the scenes, and the remaining members of the GFS formed a human curtain as they sang the refrain—this enabled each change of scene to be undertaken easily. The final verse revealed all the actors on stage illustrating their own particular needs once more, while the ' Western Nations ' slept across the table cluttered with money and possessions, completely ignoring them. . . .

' Wishing you a merry Christmas,
We will now go back to bed, sir.
Till you woke us with your knocking,
We were sleeping like the dead, sir.'

For the whole of this sequence the girls were dressed in a variety of national costumes—and we took great care that those representing the poorest countries should be dressed in very poor clothing.

The next scene was introduced by our Lord's commandment that we must love one another (from chapter 15 of St John's Gospel) which we felt was the only way in which the message of the angels, ' Peace on earth ', might eventually be achieved. At this point the girls approached the stage from the back of the church; when they reached a table they signed a treaty, shook hands, and formed a semi-circle with linked hands on the stage. This took place as the folk group sang ' Peace will Come '.

The final scene was introduced by a poem called ' A boy was born in Bethlehem ' (Janet Atkins, from *Faith, Folk, and Festivity*) followed by Philippians, chapter 2, verses 5–11. The actors joined hands and formed three circles, joining with the folk group in the song ' Let the Cosmos Ring '. We altered the words of the verses in order to make them relevant—i.e. ' By loving all the helpless '; ' By finding homes for the homeless '; etc.—and these were shouted out by a solo voice as the remainder sang ' Praise Him ', repeatedly. During this the circles of actors moved in clockwise and anti-clockwise directions, clapping their hands at appropriate points.

After the prayers and blessing, and the final congregational carol, all the actors surprised the congregation by moving among them, shaking their hands and singing, ' We wish you a merry Christmas and a happy New Year! '

The service drew a congregation of around 180, and certainly brought along quite a number of parents who would normally not have bothered to attend church at Christmas time. We hope our message was driven home.

THREE PRAYERS FOR CHRISTMAS

used by Edward Jacson during family services

Mary and Jesus

Oh God, our heavenly Father, thank you for choosing Mary to be the mother of Jesus.
Help us to learn from her to trust in you.
Give us the calm and strong outlook on life that she has.
Keep us humble as she was humble.
Help us never to be so proud nor so full of ourselves that we miss your offer to let us play our part in your plan.

Grant us the joy she had in doing your will, and the wisdom to hand over even our dearest hopes and plans and people to your care.

Thank you for Jesus and all he has done for us.
Help us to enjoy with him his birthday on Christmas Day, and so make us happy to share with him every day of our lives.

All this we ask because he came and lived and died for our sakes, and is alive again, and shows us how to love you now, and how to love each other.

Blessing the crib

Almighty God, our heavenly Father, please bless this crib, which helps us to remember how Jesus your Son, our Lord, was born in a stable at Bethlehem.

Grant that all those who remember Jesus' coming when they come to our crib, may be filled with happiness and may love you truly. Through Jesus Christ our Lord, who lives and reigns with you and the Holy Spirit for ever.

At the crib

Jesus, you were born in a stable in Bethlehem.
    Jesus, you are for everyone.

Nearby shepherds and kings from far away brought their gifts.
    Jesus, you are for everyone.

You cured both Jews and Samaritans, Romans and people from other countries.
    Jesus, you are for everyone.

Your friends were fishermen, a tax collector, a doctor, a tent-maker. Men came from many other jobs to follow you.
    Jesus, you are for everyone.

Now you have followers in all parts of the world, of many different colours and races, who worship you in their own languages.
    Jesus, you are for everyone.

Today we come, with all our differences, to worship you.
    Jesus, you are for everyone.

SEASONAL PRAYERS

by Edward Jacson

1: for young people and adults

O God our Heavenly Father, although many tragic and confusing disasters take place on this earth and affect our lives profoundly, we pray to you with hope in our hearts.

The light shines in the darkness and the darkness has not overcome it.

We thank you for sending Christ at Christmas to reassure us.

The light shines in the darkness and the darkness has not overcome it.

We pray for all people who suffer war, hatred and violence at this present time, especially in Ireland and elsewhere in the world, that they may regain national peace and personal freedom.

The light shines in the darkness and the darkness has not overcome it.

We pray for the dispirited, the disillusioned and all who can no longer make any sense out of life, that they may regain hope and personal balance and so face life anew.

The light shines in the darkness and the darkness has not overcome it.

We pray for the hungry, the homeless and all refugees, men, women and children, that the organisations set up to relieve them may be supported by all who have enough to spare, and that people may volunteer their services so that the work may go on.

The light shines in the darkness and the darkness has not overcome it.

We pray for all who are sick in hospital or at home. Especially we pray for children away from home at Christmas, for families split up and saddened by ill health and impending death of dear ones, that they may know true comfort and understanding from neighbours and friends and be filled with your Holy Spirit of strength, peace and consolation.

The light shines in the darkness and the darkness has not overcome it.

Grant to all those whose duty demands that they be at work over Christmas, the time to recall and share with their friends and relations the joy of Christmas. May they show forth in their work the patience, compassion and devotion which Christ himself came to show to all mankind when he was born on the first Christmas Day.

The light shines in the darkness and the darkness has not overcome it.

Finally we pray for ourselves, that we may be made glad by this yearly remembrance of Christ's birthday. Grant that as we celebrate with prayer, carols and the giving and receiving of presents, with good food and drink and fellowship, we may not forget that Christ was born, lived, died and rose again, in order that mankind might have hope of life for ever.

The light shines in the darkness and the darkness has not overcome it.

Thank you, God. Amen.

2: for younger children

Today is Jesus's birthday

Thank you, God, for Jesus

We remember how he was born in a stable, because there was no room for Mary and Joseph to stay in Bethlehem.

Thank you, God, for Jesus.

Bethlehem was the City of David, who was Israel's best king because he tried to do what God wanted.

Thank you, God, for Jesus.

Joseph and Mary were of the same family as King David, so the old prophets were right in saying God's son would be related to King David and born in his city.

Thank you, God, for Jesus.

The shepherds were the first people to recognise Jesus as the Son of God.

Thank you, God, for Jesus.

But they only knew who he was because a message from God had told them first of all.

Thank you, God, for Jesus.

The wise men from faraway countries travelled a long way over the desert, following a star, in order to find him, and when they saw him, they also knew him.

Thank you, God, for Jesus.

Help us to know Jesus as your Son, our friend, our Lord.

Thank you, God, for Jesus.

SO GREEN THE ASH

A folksong for Christmas by Elizabeth Hawes, intended for guitar accompaniment

A tree there was in Bethlehem
That grew beside a door
Where travellers could find a bed
And pay the inn-keeper.
The Ash was green!
So green the Ash
Upon a winter's night
When all the stars of Bethlehem
Were shining clear and bright.

As Mary lay in Bethlehem
Before her boy was born,
Her mattress was the stable straw
Among the manger corn.
The Ash was green!
So green the Ash
Upon a winter's night
When all the stars of Bethlehem
Were shining clear and bright.

Her hands and feet were frosty pale,
And while she softly wept,
Her waiting woe did undergo
And soon a baby slept.
The Ash was green!
So green the Ash
Upon a winter's night
When all the stars of Bethlehem
Were shining clear and bright.

Then Joseph broke a branch of Ash
For fire to mend the cold,
And Mary smiled to see her child
By leaping tongues of gold!
The Ash was green!
So green the Ash
That burned on Christmas morn
While Mary in the stable lay
When Jesus Christ was born.

A CAROL OF HIS COMING

Dorothy M. Bates suggests that this carol might be sung to 'The Eton Boating Song' or to some tune with a similar rhythm

This is the birth of a stranger,
The birth of a refugee.
Homeless he lies in a manger
With oxen for company.
Yet this is the world's creator,
Who was living when time began;
But into this world at Christmas
He came to live as a man.

He left the home of his glory,
His palace of light and life,
Came into our human story
Of sorrow and pain and strife.
Yet this is the world's creator
Who hung up the stars to shine;
He came to this world at Christmas,
Born into a life like mine.

That's why we're gaily singing
As we look at the Christmas tree;
That's why the bells are ringing
For Jesus' nativity.
For he is the world's creator,
Whom we worship and bless today
That his power and glory for ever
Have come to this world to stay.

Joyce Goldmanis captures the mood of

ADVENT IN A STABLE

The nights are cold and dark once more,
The stable light burns warm and dim
And as I turn the yellow straw
My thoughts run on, to him, to him . . .
To him whose cradle was the hay
Whose watchmen were the gentle kine,
Who helpless in a stable lay,
A stable old and low like mine.

The hay within the manger bars,
The pony standing peacefully,
The keen night air, the frosty stars
Foretold the Christmas mystery.
Stable, and hay, and star, and all,
(For flickering Sirius greenly burns)
Soon, soon he comes, the Babe so small,
The wondrous midnight hour returns.

And almost, ere the moment dies,
I hear the voice of cherubim,
' Your Master in the manger lies,
Bow down, bow down and worship him.'
And so, now days are cold and raw,
And Christmastide draws on apace,
At night when I put down the straw
My stable is a holy place.

(With acknowledgements to ' Riding ' magazine)

Two carols:

THE WITNESSES

by Joyce Goldmanis

Magi in kingly splendour
Travelled from lands afar,
Slowly, with toil and labour,
They followed a distant star.

Angel-directed shepherds,
Filled with deep amaze,
Hastened from fold to stable
To kneel and worship and gaze.

But animals, humble and faithful,
Dwellers in byre and stall
Found their Lord in the morning
With never a journey at all.

JESUS TODAY

by Pamela Verrall

No candles lit the stable bare,
When Jesus Christ was born.
No fires glowed to warm the air,
When Jesus Christ was born.
But there was peace when all was done,
And there was warmth, as from the sun.
And there was rest for ev'ryone,
When Jesus Christ was born.

No fond relations came to call,
When Jesus Christ was born.
No birthday cards hung in the hall,
When Jesus Christ was born.
But all the creatures, kneeling there
Breathed all their love upon the air,
And worshipped him with silent care,
When Jesus Christ was born.

If Jesus Christ were born today,
And lay in stable bare,
If Jesus Christ were born today,
And strangers came to stare,
Would you have love enough to spare,
To take him gifts and breathe a prayer?
Or would you pass without a care,
If Christ were born today?

THE HEART OF THE APPLE

A reflection for Advent by Pamela Egan

' Hell,' said the poet, ' is inaccurate.'
The converse, happily, is also true.
Creation gave us a world of pattern and shape
A rhythm of natural order,
A mesh of significances,
The endless chances to discover
That unrelated symbols
Do, in fact, astonishingly, relate.
In this Creator's world
A honeycomb sequence of transistors
And the natural mathematics of a sunflower head
Can give equal pleasure.
Poetry is made from surprising equations,
And a single apple can connect the terms
That resolve in incarnate love.

Look at the apple.
Scarlet-streaked, it hangs on a tree.
To pluck it was, once, to make a choice—
To say to God, ' No, we will do *this*.'
' Adam lay y-bounden,
Bounden in a bond . . .
And all was for an apple,
An apple that he took,
As clerkes finden written
In their Book.
Ne had the apple taken been . . .'
And had it not? What then?
Then another pattern would have begun—not ours.
Ours entailed taking the apple.

It lies in your hand now. Cut it open.
Cut it not down, but across, through the heart.
The surprising equation is made.
The symbols mesh, the terms connect.
At the heart of the apple is a star.

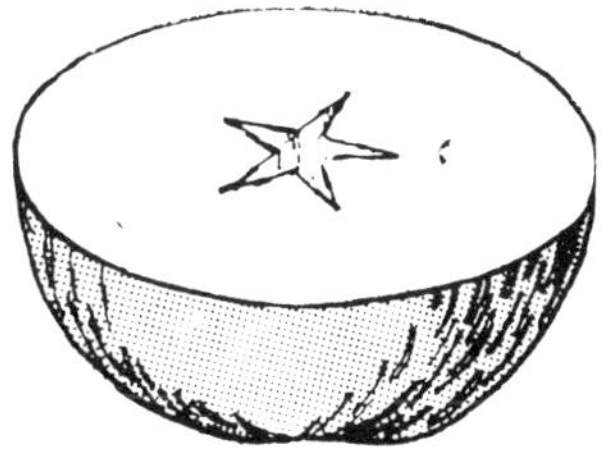

TO BETHLEHEM WITH LOVE

Try Hilda Rostron's words to a carol tune such as 'It came upon the midnight clear'

The angels went to Bethlehem a long , long time ago,
to sing their songs to Christ the King because they loved him so.

The shepherds went to Bethlehem a long, long time ago,
to kneel beside the sleeping Babe because they loved him so.

The Wise Men went to Bethlehem a long, long time ago,
to bring him precious gifts and gold because they loved him so.

I cannot go to Bethlehem as they did long ago;
but I *can* sing my carol now because I love him so.

POINT OF NO RETURNING

Noel Connell reflects on the moment when the world was changed for ever

There was no place, they said, no proper haven;
No bed for tired travellers, with their dreams,
No time for pause, no moment for reflection,
To think on promises; to ponder themes.

A quiet corner was enough for Mary,
A star above, a kind word close at hand;
No other town but Bethlehem was chosen
No splendid palace in the promised land.

No royal purple for a king's occasion,
At first no notice but a sleeping sound;
A breath of heaven in an infant murmur,
A tiny hand and voice, extended down.

Across the quiet hills three kings came riding
To kneel, in joy, before a greater throne
Of wood, and swaddling cloth, and wonder;
Here in the warmth of heaven's affection born.

The holy Child, for whom the minds of angels
Inquired no more, but worshipped him in awe;
And time stood still; one point of no returning,
One glorious moment—one eternal now.

THREE CHRISTMAS SONGS

by Alison Adcock

(Tune ' There stands a little man in the woods alone ' from Humperdinck's *Hansel and Gretel*)

Our shoes and socks each morning we fill with feet,
And then about our work we go down the street.
Christmas time a marvel brings,
Filling these most common things
With unexpected treasures and joys full sweet.

The ox and donkey find in the stall their hay;
They eat it and get strength for another day.
At the earliest Christmastide
They a miracle espied,
For a little child in their manger lay.

Now children they are born every night and day,
Ordinary common things like socks and hay.
But this child is magic bread,
When on him the world is fed
All its fears and sorrows will flee away.

(Tune ' Tannenbaum ')

Our Christmas tree is evergreen,
Bright and plenteous is its fruit.
Its top in highest heaven is seen;
Deep within this earth its root.

Christ the star that crowns the tree;
We are all its shining fruit.
The church it is our Christmas tree,
Best of trees beyond dispute.

(Tune ' Gentle Jesus ' by Martin Shaw)

Jesus, be my holly tree,
Ever living, strong and tall.
Like the ivy, close to thee
I shall climb and never fall.

By one Spirit both are fed,
Twining ivy, springing tree,
I by winding pathways tread;
Straight and strong thou leadest me.

So to heaven we grow apace
Rooted deep in faith and love.
Prop and guide, I thee embrace.
And by thee find light above.

A SIMPLE CRIB

Maureen Norton shows a crib design which can be made on any scale—large for a group project, small for the child's own 'take home' work

We now come to the heart of the Christmas festival. I have planned a crib which can be made in various sizes; either the whole class could work on one as a group, or individual older juniors, whose fingers are nippier, could make one each, to take home and keep in a place of honour.

The actual size depends on the size of the cardboard box used for the stable itself. Soap, cereals, etc. are often delivered to your local shop in boxes of various useful sizes. Make sure that the figures will be to scale when the scene is finished.

For materials you will need, as well as the box, coloured paper (bits of old wallpaper will do very well), the cardboard core of a toilet roll, glue and sharp scissors or a safety razor.

Draw an outline on the outside of the box as in fig. 1, and then cut away what you will not want (fig. 2). In this way the box will give you a good basic shape for the stable, and you can then surround it with greenery and straw. To make the manger for a small crib, cut one slice from the end of the toilet roll core, and then cut

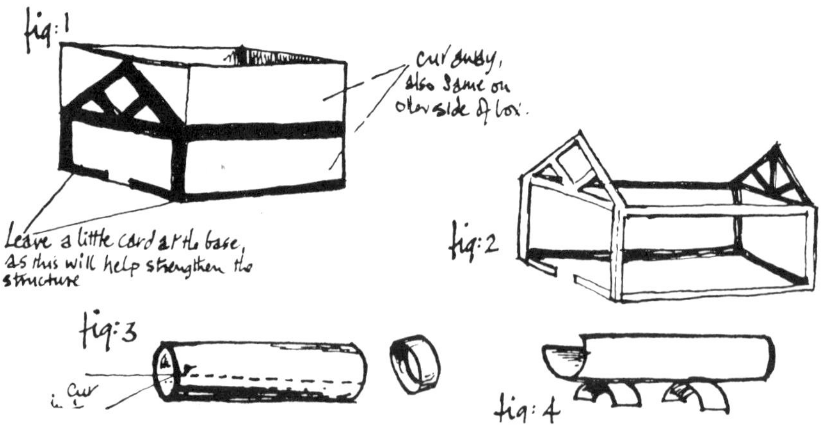

the rest of the roll in half lengthways (fig. 3). Now cut the slice in half, too, and use these two little bits for the feet, just by glueing them to the main body (fig. 4). A larger manger can be made from a rectangular cardboard box, suitably painted or covered with scraps of wood-grain pattern adhesive paper. Fill the manger with fine packing straw or shavings (usually not hard to come by at this time of year) or with very finely shredded paper. For the Baby, it is better to use a tiny doll than to try to make a paper figure.

When making the other figures, don't worry about putting features on the faces. It is just as effective, if not even more so, to leave them off altogether, and many of the best modern religious pictures for children often do this. Contrary to what we might expect, it does not seem to worry the child, whose eye prefers the simple shape to a mass of detail. All the figures are based on the simple cone shape—just a section cut from a circle of stiff paper or card. For fig. 5, cut out the hands and arms as shown, and fix to the back of the cone. From different-coloured paper, cut out a cape, fold at the neck and place over the cone. Glue the head (a small paper cylinder) to the cape at the top of the cone. Cut a strip of paper into a fringe at both ends for the hair, add a crown, and glue into his hands either a casket or a small cake candle.

Figs. 6 and 7 are made in a similar way, though fig 6 has a pleated cone as a base. Glue on his arms first, then his robe, with the square piece at the back and the stole-like ends in front. As a variant, fig. 7 can be made from a cylinder rather than a cone, with a cone-shaped robe, stuck to the top of the cylinder. Mary should have a blue cape (fig. 8), and can have a simple gold disc for a halo, to which the head is stuck—or it can be cut from one piece of gold paper and fixed separately to the figure (fig. 9). These are very easy, basic ideas, but the children will enjoy decorating the figures, and the final shapes, though stylised, are bold enough to be striking and satisfying.

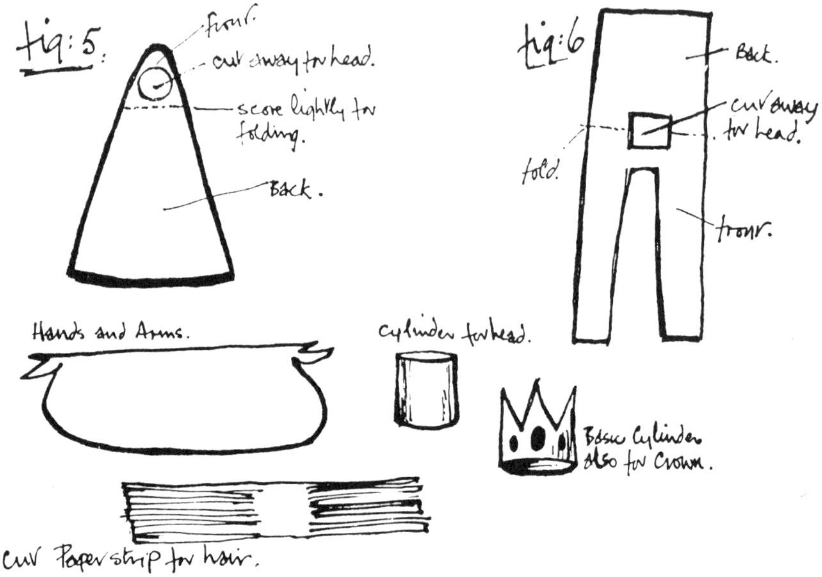
fig:5.
front.
cut away for head.
score lightly for folding.
Back.
fig:6
Back.
cut away for head.
fold.
front.
Hands and Arms.
cylinder for head.
Basic Cylinder also for Crown.
cut Paper strip for hair.

fig:8.
Pattern for cape

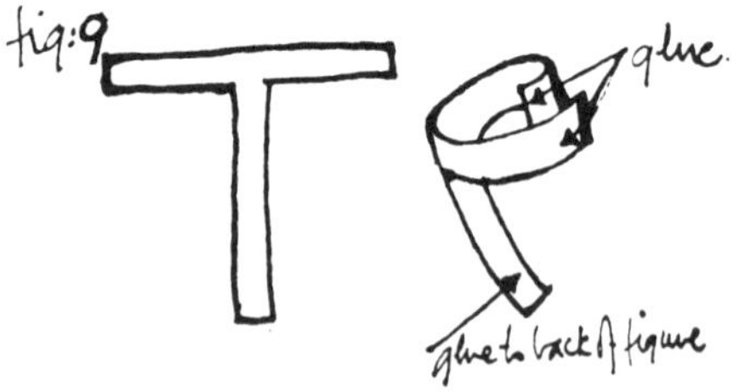
fig:9
glue.
glue to back of figure

CRAFTS FOR CHRISTMAS

Leslie Edwards has encouraged his class to make all the things he writes about

One of the easiest shapes from which to make a Christmas decoration is a star. Stars can be cut from foil paper and stuck in pairs with a string running down between them, until you have enough strings to hang round a lampshade or light fitting; they can be fastened to walls or windows, or used to make place cards at parties, and even the smallest will find pleasure in making their own and frosting them with glitter. The diagrams in Figure 1, page 118, can be copied for a basic shape. If two stars are cut to the same size, one can be slit to the centre and the other fitted into it at right-angles, to give a 3-D effect. These stars can be cut from thin card of different colours, or white card sprayed with coloured lacquer or paint.

Take-home Christmas cards are very popular. One variation on the usual shape is to draw a picture inside the folded paper, where you usually find the greeting. Then cut two doors into the outside cover, so that when the doors are opened, you can see the picture. The greeting can be written on the doors (Figures 2a and 2b). If the picture is drawn on the outside, perhaps it could be cut round to make a card with an interesting shape (Figure 2c). A very simple church window design can be made by folding the card as usual, and cutting shapes out of the front piece to suggest the window. These can be backed with coloured paper—bright foil paper is ideal.

Many of the suggestions which follow for calendars can also be adapted for cards, so there is no need for any child to go home this Christmas with the same sort of card he took last year.

Calendars

There are basically two sorts of simple calendar. The date-pad can be hung on the card below the picture (Figures 3a and 3b) or stuck on the card (Figure 3c). The card itself can be cut into a simple shape, using a template if necessary, and the date-pad fastened on to it or underneath. The shape can be decided by the interests of the children. Ships, rockets and houses are always popular.

A card can be folded to stand up horizontally, and a shape cut out and stuck on top of it (Figure 3d). Interesting work for older or more able children is to use silhouettes. Cut a shape from white paper and put it on to black card. No detail is necessary, but the shape must be clear. Perhaps there is some interesting building near the child's home or church which just asks to be treated in this way; it is always a popular plan to use somewhere known to the children, and to the recipient. More interesting still is to cut the shape carefully from white paper, using that piece of paper to make the card, and then to colour the cut-out shape and stick it inside the card, so that it can be seen through the hole.

For walls and ceilings

A pleasant ' abstract ' decoration can be made by putting coloured drinking straws into balls of Plasticine and hanging them from the ceiling. Ordinary uncoloured straws are cheaper, but should be lacquered or painted before use. They can be hung simply by threading thin string through the ball and knotting it underneath (Figure 4).

Large, cheerful wall decorations can be made in the shape of choirboys beginning with the basic shape (Figure 5a) cut from scarlet paper or felt. All that needs to be added is feet, head and a ' surplice ' made from a paper doyley or pleated white crêpe paper. Smaller versions of this design can of course be made into cards or calendars. Older children might enjoy making song-books, lanterns, etc. which could stand out to give a 3-D effect.

For windows, tissue paper is excellent, because it allows the light to shine through. In the day, light shines from outside and the picture looks pleasant from within fhe room; at night the effect is gained from outside. This double effect should always be remembered and the pictures placed accordingly. Very simple abstract pictures are made by cutting or tearing pieces out of thick dark paper and covering the holes carefully with tissue paper of different colours. When the children understand the principle, they can make pictures to illustrate the Christmas story, or carols and Christmas songs. The important thing to remember is that the part cut out will be the important bit; the rest is background. Detail should be avoided. All that is necessary is a suggestion.

An idea for a tissue paper picture

Another outline suitable for tissue paper pictures

Wall Pictures

Large pictures for the Sunday school building or the church porch may be made by tearing figures from coloured paper and sticking them on to a different-coloured background. In this work scissors should not be used. The rough edges give emphasis to the total picture. To be effective, these pictures must be big. It is best to allow the children to work out for themselves the meaning of Christmas, and to express themselves as they wish; never mind if Mary is wearing a wig 'like Mummy', or Jesus has a panda in his cot.

Older children can copy in felt-pen a suitable text from the Bible, or the verse of a carol, illuminating the first letter as monks did in their manuscripts (Figure 6). This could be done in really big, bold script. If there is an accessible window in the church entrance, this is an excellent place for a tissue-paper picture or a window painting with powder paint put directly on to the glass.

Presents

Simple presents which young children can give to their parents afford great satisfaction to all, even in these sophisticated days.

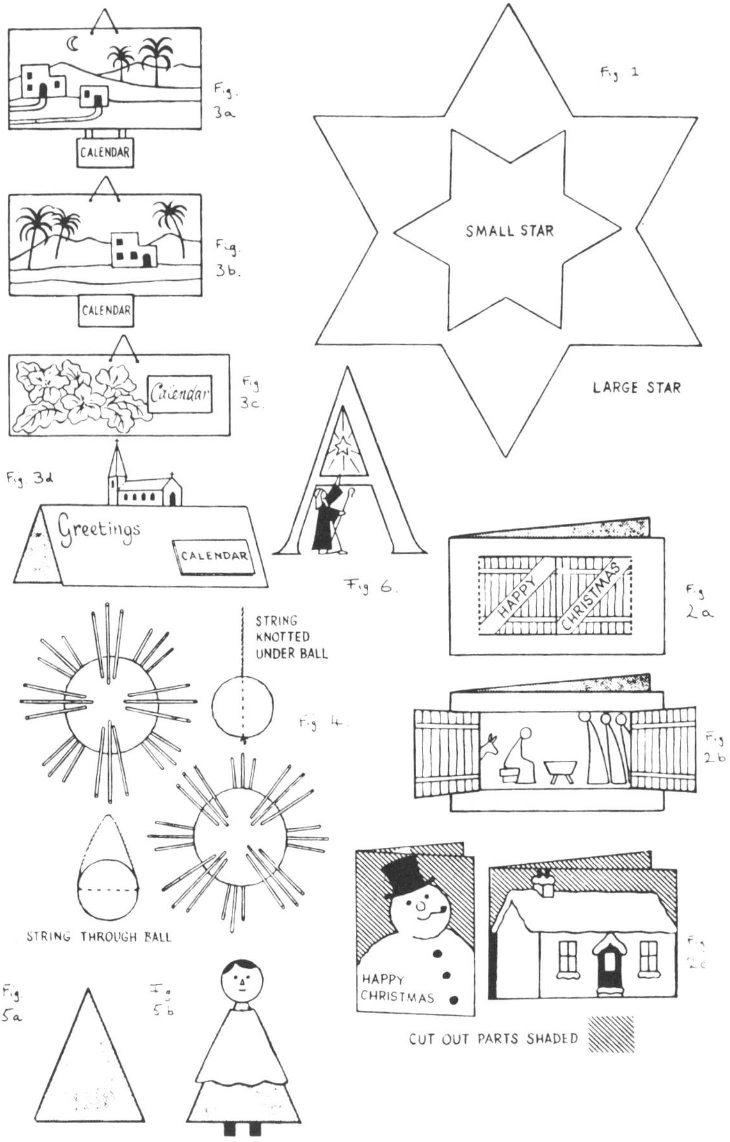

A wooden spoon can be made into a key-holder for Mum to keep in the kitchen. Make a face on the back of the spoon with beads and reinforcement rings, glued on, and add wool 'hair'. Screw cup hooks into the handle to hold the keys, and a small round hook into the back of the bowl, so that the spoon can be hung up.

A useful pot for Dad to put things in can be made from a tin, washed and covered with tiny pieces of paper torn from coloured magazines, to give a mosaic effect. Gummed paper can also be used. Perhaps one tin could be labelled 'Nails' and another 'Screws'. Brothers and sisters could be given tins intended for pencil-holders or hairpins, etc. If the brother or sister has a particular interest, for instance gardening, then the child can make a suitable picture on a card and attach a small packet of seeds to the card.

All that has been suggested in this article is meant to stimulate interest and initiative. If you originally set out to follow a design suggested here, you may find that the child has added his own idea and the final product is nothing like what you had in mind. Don't worry! Art and craft are such personal things that children as well as adults like to express themselves in their own way, according to their own ability and estimate of what is pleasing and worthwhile. If, however, these suggestions are followed exactly, the children should still be happy with what they have done, because each suggestion has been tried with children who have enjoyed them.